Getting to Justice

Marilia, So pleased that you will read my book.

Faith Ireland
9-17-24

Getting to Justice: From Unwed Mother to the State Supreme Court

© Copyright 2024 by Faith Ireland.

Written by Faith Ireland.
Development editing by Steve Peha.
Proofreading and copy editing by Mallory Benson.
Layout and design by Steve Peha.

All rights reserved. Permission to reproduce or transmit in any form or by any means, electronic or mechanical, including photocopying and recording, or by an information storage and retrieval system, (including but not limited to the Internet), must be secured in writing from the publisher.

Printed in the United States of America.

Published by:

Faith Ireland
www.faith-ireland.com

ISBN: 979-8-218-40261-7

Getting to Justice

From Unwed Mother to the State Supreme Court

by

Faith Ireland

Contents

Preface 7
Introduction 9
1. Not Your Average Twelve-Year-Old Girl 13
2. College Daze 25
3. What's the Worst That Could Happen? 35
4. In a Family Way 45
5. Is Law School Still Possible? 59
6. Clearing the Bar 75
7. The First of Many Firsts 85
8. New Friends, New Experiences 99
9. Kim 113
10. Discoveries 131
11. Taking a Chance on Love 145
12. An Ending and a Beginning 161
13. Stepping Up 177
14. What Kind of Justice? 189
15. Always Running 199
16. Pain and Promise 209
17. Once Bitten, Twice Shy? 219
18. Getting to Justice 233

Preface

In this book, I share deeply personal experiences and the most important life lessons I've learned. I would like to acknowledge my parents, Janice and Carl Enyeart, and my two brothers, Pat and Tim, who gave so much of their lives to me. I would also like to thank my husband, Chuck Norem, and my birth daughter, Emily Cantrell, who have given me so much to live for.

Writing a memoir obviously requires recollection. Looking back as far as seven decades, I'm gratified to have recollected so much. At the same time, I recognize that what I remember now may not be exactly what I experienced way back when.

I learned this particular life lesson when I was a Superior Court Judge in King County, WA, and a controversial expert witness, psychologist Dr. Elizabeth Loftus, testified in my court about the unreliability of human memory. Her research, captured in the book *Memory: Surprising New Insights into How We Remember and Why We Forget*, showed that we are apt to misremember many things, even things we feel absolutely certain of. Apparently, the human brain isn't the reliable source of truth we think it is.

I write this book for you and for me. To you, I want to give the many keys to a long and happy life that have been given to me by people who wrote to empower others. Many of these lessons you will have heard before. You'll think: "I already know that." But are you using it in your life? You aren't the same person today that you were when you first learned these things.

I'm not the same person, either. This is why I write for myself: to cherish what I've learned, to thank the people I've learned from, and to remind myself of the best lessons from my past so that I can bring them with me into the present and on to the future.

My mother had two sons when she became pregnant with me. She said she absolutely knew that her third child would be a girl. Because my mother had faith, that became my name.

The word "faith" is sometimes described as belief without proof. I do not claim scientific accuracy in this memoir. I offer recollections to share the ups and downs of a life well lived and what I've learned along the way. My hope is that some of the lessons I've learned will be lessons you can learn from too.

I began writing at fifteen as a high school journalist and continued to study journalism in college. While a member of the Washington State Supreme Court, I wrote dozens of opinions. I have also written for many legal books.

All of this work has been grounded in facts that served as proof of my beliefs and those of many others. But this book is different. It requires belief without proof. Welcome to my world.

—Faith Ireland, June 21, 2024

Introduction

By Anne Bremner, Trial Attorney and On-Air Legal Analyst

Faith has been a source of wisdom, guidance, and friendship for almost forty years. I met Faith in the mid-1980s when I was prosecuting a high-profile murder case in her courtroom, and she served as a member of the King County Superior Court. But I had seen and heard about her before that.

A few years earlier, fresh out of law school, I was clerking for Judge Robert E. Dixon, a much-loved member of the bench known for his fairness and compassion. One day, Judge Dixon told me a woman was being sworn into the court, and I should attend the ceremony.

At that time, you could count the number of female superior court judges on one hand. Even in the 1980s, seeing a woman in this position was rare. One of those rare women was Faith.

How rare? I could fill a book with all I have to say about her. But you're about to read that book, so I'll leave these discoveries to you.

Later in my career, I engaged Faith as a coach and consultant. I was arguing the largest, most important case of my life. I knew I needed support and who I wanted to get it from. But I had yet to learn how comprehensive that support would be.

Working with Faith in her coaching program was nothing like I expected—and everything I needed it to be. As you'll see in this book, she has a real gift for asking the right questions at the right time and pushing the people she cares about to answer them.

That's the thing about Faith: she's so focused, detail-oriented, and disciplined in her approach. She was always asking me: What do you want? What are the steps you need to get there? And then, when I returned, she'd ask: Did you take those steps? Where are you now? What do you need to do next?

Faith was a taskmaster, but she also helped me complete those tasks. I never felt alone when I was working with her; she was right there with me every step of the way.

And she didn't just help me in my professional life. Faith's coaching is holistic. She knows there's more to being happy and successful than conquering the challenges of one's career.

She helped me address issues related to friends, family, colleagues, health, even spirituality. She knows how complicated life can be and how important it is to address the needs of the whole person, to consider all factors as she guides her clients in making decisions, setting goals, and taking action toward achieving them.

Faith has always been the perfect coach for me, as I know she's been for many others. But I realized a long time ago that she offers more than coaching; she offers mentoring as well.

Mentoring matters greatly to Faith. It's how she gives back and how she leaves her mark on the world. It's how she leans into her work as a coach and how she lives into the wonder of being a part of something larger than herself.

If there's an answer to the question of why Faith is so good at what she does, you'll find it here in these pages. In this unusual collection of more than 150 life experiences, she grows from a 12-year-old girl with societally unacceptable career goals to becoming a member of The Washington State Supreme Court. Through it all, she breaks boundaries, blazes trails, and perseveres through tragedy time and again.

Faith is the real thing. If you're going through something, chances are she's gone through it, too. And she's not afraid to talk about it. She's among the most honest, open, and forthright people I've ever known.

One thing you can be certain of is that Faith is not in this work for her ego. If she talks about herself, it's only because she wants you to see that no matter what you're going through, she's gone through something like it.

She's made it through with perseverance, hard work, and I guess I'd have to say with faith—in you, in herself, in life, and in the Universe. As John Lennon said, "Everything will be OK in the end. If it's not OK, it's not the end." I think that's how Faith looks at life, too.

As you read this book, you'll see Faith in situations where life is not OK. There are many of these moments; pay close attention to how she deals with them. I'm sure you'll see as I have that some of the keys to success and happiness in her life are a strong sense of ownership, the courage to be vulnerable and ask for help, a willingness to change and do the hard work that change requires, and plain old perseverance until she gets what she's been wanting.

Faith has experienced big wins in her life and just as many tragic losses. How does she keep going? How does she move forward to the next success when most of us would wallow in self-pity? How does she make her life work when the world is working against her?

The answers are in these pages. May you find getting to know Faith as instructive, entertaining, and inspirational as I have.

—Anne Bremner, June 25, 2024

1
CHAPTER ONE

Not Your Average Twelve-Year-Old Girl

If I Were a Boy

It's 1954. I'm 12. I'm watching the Army-McCarthy Hearings on black-and-white TV with Mom and Dad.

Senator McCarthy says there's a "Communist under every bed." For four years, he's been saying he has a list of the names of over two hundred Communists in the federal government. But we've never seen or heard the names. He just takes the list out of his pocket once in a while, reads it silently to himself, and shakes it at us.

This is the first time McCarthy's investigation is on TV for all to see. He claims the military is littered with Communists. I see the damage he's doing to people right before my twelve-year-old eyes.

My state of Washington starts its own investigation into alleged Communists. A woman in her forties, the owner of Ethel's Apparel, a small women's clothing store we shop at regularly, is accused of having been a Communist in the 1920s. Although nothing is proven, the mere allegation ruins her business, which is forced to close.

My parents are civic-minded, patriotic, liberal. Dad served in World War II and Korea. He's outraged by the allegations. I, too, am angry. The unfairness of it all is obvious, even to a twelve-year-old girl.

I say to Mom and Dad, "If I were a boy, I could be a lawyer." My parents sit silent. They know girls can't be lawyers. I know that too. But what I also know is that lawyers help people who are falsely accused. That's what I'm going to do.

Nothing is impossible. Some things are just less likely than others.
—*Jonathan Winters*

Two Things I'll Never Be

Even though Mr. Simmons teaches math, which is not my favorite subject, he's my favorite teacher because he tells exciting stories of his travels around the world.

But he's not my teacher now. He's my eighth-grade counselor.

I've completed my proficiency tests. They're supposed to help me determine which courses to take in high school.

Mr. Simmons talks generally about my scores without showing them to me. I think I know what he's about to say. And I know I don't want to hear it.

"Your scores in language arts and social studies are very good," he says. "But in math and science, they're low."

Mr. Simmons looks uncomfortable, but I'm not hurt. I've been told all my life that I can't do math and science, and part of me believes it. But part of me thinks I can. Mom's a realtor. She does math, so I'm hopeful.

Mr. Simmons talks about careers for girls: secretary, teacher, nurse. He advises me to take typing and shorthand because he thinks secretary is the best choice for me. Becoming a teacher or a nurse would require college. He says I'm "not college material" and then excuses me to go to class.

It's not news to me that I struggle in math and science. The only time I use numbers is for a pattern when I'm sewing or in the kitchen for recipes. Even then, it doesn't come easy. Science is agonizing. Trying to memorize atoms and particles makes me crazy.

I haven't thought about college. No one in my family has a degree. Mom started but dropped out during her first year when she found a job as a secretary, a rare prize in the Depression.

Mom's in real estate now. Among five salespeople, she's the only woman. Dad likes to joke: "Your mom can't do math either. Unless she's figuring out her commission for a sale."

Dad went to work after sixth grade. He says he's still in school—the school of hard knocks.

I babysit for men who are pilots, doctors, and lawyers. But only one of the wives works.

I'll work when I'm older. But not as a lawyer because there are two things I'll never be: a college graduate and a boy.

Whether you think you can or think you can't, you're right.
—Henry Ford

Nonsense!

It's the summer of 1956. I'm babysitting for Bob Greive, our state senator. Babysitting is the only job available for a fourteen-year-old girl. My brother Tim is fifteen. He's worked at a grocery store for two years. He makes three times what I make per hour. My brother Pat is a senior in high school and makes excellent money as a salesman in an exclusive men's clothing store near the University of Washington.

Senator Greive is also our family attorney. Mom was rear-ended last year. He's helping her get fair compensation for her injuries.

While the kids play outside, I stuff envelopes for the senator's campaign. Politics fascinates me. I regularly attend Democratic meetings with my parents and help Dad, a precinct committeeman, distribute campaign literature.

The senator asks me about my college plans.

"Oh, I'm not going," I say. "I was told I'm not college material."

"Nonsense!" he replies. "Get started on your prerequisites."

The moment he says, "Nonsense!" I know I can do it. He believes in me.

Algebra and chemistry. Ugh! I feel defeated. But there's something else I feel, too: a sense of possibility.

Senator Greive is straightforward and direct. He's our newest senate majority leader, an astute politician known for being outspoken. This gets him in trouble in the legislature, but he's respected for his honesty and his commitment to living the courage of his convictions.

I also know his voting record. He was one of the few legislators who voted against the formation of a state committee tasked with Communist witch-hunting.

Besides, I hate shorthand. Even though Mr. Simmons said I should become a secretary, I haven't for a minute wanted to be one.

College prep courses will be hard, but they'll be much more interesting.

Senator Greive thinks I *am* college material. He's the only person, other than Mom and Dad, who's had this much faith in me—more faith, even, than I've had in myself.

Who have you believed who said, "You can?"

Quadratic Equations and Logarithms

As she dusts and irons clothes, Mom listens to a book—*Think and Grow Rich* by Napoleon Hill—on a long-play record. She wants to learn more about how to be a successful realtor.

Following the advice Senator Greive gave me last year, I'm taking algebra, a college prerequisite.

Senator Greive believes I can be a college graduate. Little by little, I'm starting to believe it too. But on many days, doubt overwhelms me. Quadratic equations and logarithms drive me crazy.

We're in the middle of a major remodel to our home overlooking Puget Sound with a western view of Vashon, Blake, and Bainbridge Islands. The addition will give us a large family room, an adjoining expanded kitchen with a wood-burning stove, and an added bedroom and bath.

The addition is costly, but Mom knows it will increase the value of our home. Dad, a plumber and pipefitter, does much of the work, but other contractors are required. He's even more excited than Mom about the potential increase in value.

In general, Dad is more optimistic; Mom is more realistic. I see how different they are but also how they complement each other. I know that I benefit from both of them.

I still lack the confidence I need to succeed. But I'm learning to hold within my mind my parents' differing perspectives. I think this will help me overcome my challenges. College or not, quadratic equations and logarithms or not, this is a time in my life when I realize how fortunate I am to have the parents I have.

My brothers groan when Mom plays the record, but I'm intrigued. Can we really think the right things and become rich? Can we control our thoughts that way? Even if we can, how do thoughts lead to things that happen in our lives? And what about negative thoughts? Does thinking that bad things will happen lead to tragedy? I'm full of questions and confusion. But mostly curiosity.

It seems to me that thoughts fall upon us like rain in Seattle, whenever and wherever. One minute, I'm thinking about a peanut butter and jelly sandwich. The next minute, I'm concerned about the Cold War and whether Russia will drop the bomb on us. But I seem to know that if I learn to direct my thinking, this ability will matter in more ways than merely making money—or conquering quadratic equations and logarithms.

What we think, we become.—Buddha

Stories

Mom and Dad take the Dale Carnegie course based on his book *How to Win Friends and Influence People*. Mom thinks it helps her in real estate. Dad's planning to become a realtor too. He wants to help Mom when he's not working as a plumbing inspector.

They quickly become teaching assistants and get me into the course for free. I'm the only high school student in the group.

They say the course will help me see myself in a new light, that it will help me develop more courage and confidence. I'm excited to attend but also nervous because everyone has to give a five-minute speech.

Mom tells me she's learned that the secret to getting people to like you is being interested in them. That doesn't sound too hard.

I become an editor of the school newspaper so I can pick my own stories. I want to write about other students. Out of the five hundred I have to choose from, I pick those who've accomplished something, those with interesting stories to tell, those I want as friends.

Interviewing is easy; it's just asking questions. And each person I interview becomes a new friend, someone who'll say "Hi!" to me as I walk between classes, someone I can sit next to at lunch.

I interview our basketball team's star player. Like the other kids I interview, he enjoys the story I write about him.

Later, someone tells me that they overheard his mother, an English teacher, saying to another teacher that I just want to date him, that I must be looking for a husband.

That's a ridiculous story. I have no intention of marrying young. Besides, he's tall and skinny and has a pimply face.

Listening is a magnetic and strange thing, a creative force. The friends who listen to us are the ones we move toward.—Karl A. Menninger

Looking for Information, I Find a Mentor

January 1960. My senior year of high school. I participate in a program about racial discrimination, particularly apartheid in South Africa. I learn that apartheid is an authoritarian political culture that ensures that South Africa is dominated politically, socially, and economically by the nation's minority white population.

I find this unbelievable and perverse.

I decide to write a term paper on apartheid. But I can't find enough information about it.

Mom has recently been appointed Education Director at the State Department of Licensing by Governor Rosellini. Her background as a pioneering woman in the real estate business helped her secure this prestigious position.

To help me with my paper, she tells me to come to the office where Wing Luke, an attorney we know, will find something for me.

Wing is one of the few Asian lawyers in Washington. He's an assistant attorney general in the civil rights division. I've met him at events in the Asian community, where my parents and I are very active. He's also attended open house events at our home in Shorewood.

I arrive with Mom at Wing's office. I'm not sure how Mom knows he can help me. I can't think of anyone who would have information on apartheid. But sure enough, Wing goes to his closet, filled with neatly arranged boxes, and quickly retrieves three papers for me. He also offers good advice. Finally, I feel like I have what I need.

The articles are excellent. Not easy to digest, but I work my way through them. My professor is impressed with my paper and asks me to present it to the class.

This is the first time Wing Luke has mentored me. But it will not be the last.

Who have your mentors been? Who are you mentoring?

Possible Presidents and the Prom

The County Democratic Party is having a high school speech contest. Mom thinks I should enter.

"But it's only a week away," I screech. "I can't get ready that fast!"

"Well," she huffs. "I know you can if you *want* to."

She's daring me. And because we've both taken the Dale Carnegie course, she knows I'll take her up on it.

A week later, I arrive nervous and excited to give my speech on why a Democratic president should be elected in 1960. Taking the dare pays off. I win. Then again, I'm the only one who shows up.

A week later, I collect my prize: the chance to compete in the state playoffs and a room at the Davenport Hotel for the Democratic State Convention in Spokane.

This time, I have many competitors. A poised and articulate speaker from Port Angeles, who has memorized her speech and delivers it without notes, blows me away.

I thought the speech was supposed to be extemporaneous. No one had given me the rules. Still, I'm quite happy with second place; my well-prepared opponent goes on to the National Convention.

One of the judges is Herb Kaplow, a nationally known TV journalist. I watch him on the nightly news all the time. Mr. Kaplow praises me for my presentation and offers a few pointers. I tell him about my interest in journalism. He takes me under his wing for the rest of the day.

Mr. Kaplow and I attend the press conferences of all the Democratic presidential candidates. I meet Hubert Humphrey, Stuart Symington, and Lyndon Johnson.

The press conference for my personal favorite, Senator John F. Kennedy, is held in his suite at the Davenport. It's standing room only. I squeeze in next to his golf clubs about fifteen feet away from the handsome candidate.

Another golfing president? I worry.

But hearing Kennedy's ideals, wit, and enthusiasm fills me with hope for our future. I'm certain he'll be our next president.

At the end of the day, Dad takes my bags to the car for the five-hour drive back to Seattle. When we pull into our driveway, Rich, my date for the senior prom, waits patiently for me in his '57 Bel Air, wearing a striking white tux. I have my hair in rollers.

I dash into the house, shower, and pull on my daffodil-yellow chiffon ball gown. Even with my handsome date, the senior prom seems anticlimactic after my day in Spokane listening to possible presidents.

Where you are in five years depends on who you meet today!
—George Stamatis

2
CHAPTER TWO

College Daze

Finding My Spot

June 1960. I'm so nervous about my grades that I wait until I get my diploma before applying for college.

Getting into the University of Washington, packed as it is with almost thirty thousand students, is competitive. Priority goes to those who have a diploma from an accredited high school. Fortunately, mine is.

Those math and science classes were dull and difficult for me. Chemistry was more interesting because we got to do something in the lab assignments instead of just memorizing facts. Math was maddening.

I'm accepted by the University of Washington for the fall quarter of 1960. I can pay the tuition with the money I've saved from babysitting.

The university is a sprawling place, large and intimidating. I want to stay on campus so I can find my way around. But because I applied late, there are no dorm rooms left, except for girls who drop out of rush.

I have no interest in being a sorority girl. But I'm going through rush anyway. I'll join a sorority if I have to, but I'd rather get a spot in the dorms. My friend Deannie Dunbar is also going through rush. She's smart and kind, a perfect friend to have right now, and someone I'm glad to room with.

Rush is a depressing three days for me. I feel like I'm being judged on my looks, my clothes, and which sorority girls I know. (I know none.)

There are so many rules about what sorority girls can and can't do. It seems to me like blind conformity. I'm more independent. Besides, I can't measure up to these smart, talented, pretty girls who know what sororities are all about.

Deannie receives three invitations; I receive none. At least I get a spot in the dorms so I can live on campus. It's more expensive than living at home, but Mom and Dad are willing to help with the extra cost. They know, just as I do, that the commute by bus from our home in Burien each day—over two hours round trip—would just be too much.

Have you ever felt left out but happy about it?

Dorm Rats

Walking between classes, I run into a few sorority girls who recognize me. They're friends of my older brother Pat. When he was going here last year, he was in a fraternity.

One of the sorority girls says to me, "Why didn't you let them know your brother was a Theta? You would've been a legacy and been able to join automatically."

Girls who went to the city high schools knew all about sororities. I went to school in middle-class Burien, south of Seattle, down by the airport. In Burien, going to college was not what families expected of their children. We certainly didn't have sorority girls visiting us.

After rush, I have no regrets. I'm glad I didn't know about legacies. I'm certain now that I wouldn't have wanted to be in a sorority.

One of my best friends, Sallie Winquist, is in the dorm room next to me. Our friend Deannie comes to hang out with us "dorm rats," as we're known. She's not even sure she wants to continue living in her sorority. She's even thinking about changing schools.

I don't want to belong to any club that will accept me as a member.
—Groucho Marx

Divide and Conquer

I struggle in college, especially in history where, rather than having regular assignments, I have one paper that determines my grade.

I feel strongly that child labor laws are inadequate even today. So I choose the history of child labor as my topic.

With a three-inch-tall stack of three-by-five cards, I have more information than I can handle, and I don't know what to do.

My boyfriend, Hayes Elder, is in law school. I met him when he worked on Senator Greive's staff.

He meets me in the library to help me with my paper. Seeing my towering stack of cards, he poses a question: "If you were to divide that stack in half, what would your topic be?"

"Child labor in England," I reply.

"And if you divided it again?"

We play this game until my stack is manageable.

I write my paper on "Child Labor in England from 1890 to 1900." I get an A.

I now know how to produce A papers in the future.

Riding the roller coaster of my academic self-confidence, I think I might be college material after all.

Do you ever make a project bigger than it needs to be?

Politics in Person

The envelope-stuffing I started when I was babysitting for Senator Greive leads to other opportunities in politics. I'm part of a team of four now, led by Hayes, the senator's assistant.

Senator Greive has us working for a Democratic candidate in a legislative district where we can truly make a difference. We review public voting records by precinct. We designate the precincts as Red (Democrat), Blue (Republican), Orange (neutral, leaning Democrat), or Green (neutral, leaning Republican). Then, in the orange and green precincts, we doorbell with our candidate's literature.

Weeks of hard work pay off; we're very successful. As a result, Senator Greive offers me a job at the State Legislature in Olympia for the 1961 legislative term. This isn't a volunteer page job for high school kids. I don't know what I'll be doing, but I know it pays well.

I'm excited about this, especially because Hayes will be there too. I'll need to take a quarter off from college, but I want the experience.

From my volunteer work with the senator and the State Democratic Committee, I already know a lot about the election process. When I return to school for the spring quarter, I'll know even more.

Seeing politics in person is much better than reading about it in the paper. I'll have an advantage—perhaps even over my political science professor.

Every job you ever have will build you, whether it's volunteering, babysitting, flipping burgers, or working in the State Senate.

Someone Thinks I Should Go to Law School

In the spring of 1962, Wing Luke takes a leave of absence from the attorney general's office to run for Seattle City Council. I'm excited by his daring.

As a campaign volunteer, I accompany him to a political event in Tacoma. I marvel at the beautiful sunset as we approach the city.

"Isn't that sunset lovely?" I say.

Wing corrects me. "What you're seeing is pollution," he says.

Pollution! I feel depressed.

Soon, the smell of Tacoma's pulp and paper mill hits us with its putrid odor of rotten eggs. It's called the "Aroma of Tacoma."

I've been seeing more articles about the environment in the newspapers lately. If I want to be in politics and do more than pass out brochures, this is an issue I need to pay attention to.

Wing is the most qualified candidate for the position he seeks, but I'm nervous about the voters. If elected, he'd be the first Asian city council member in Seattle. Are people ready for this?

Wing is a war hero. He received a Bronze Star Medal for his service in Korea and the South Pacific. He has a BA in political science and public administration and a law degree from the University of Washington. As we near the event, Wing encourages me to pursue a law degree. I'm smiling as we arrive.

Clean air is a basic right. The responsibility to ensure that falls to Congress and the president.—Tom Carper

A Landslide Victory

Wing Luke runs a campaign emphasizing the need for fairness in housing. As an assistant attorney general, he fought to prohibit discrimination in the selling or renting of real estate. This is what motivated him to run. He also promotes Native American fishing rights, urban renewal, and historic preservation.

Receiving 30,000 votes more than his competitor, Wing wins by a landslide.

I attend his swearing-in ceremony as he becomes the first Asian American to hold elected office in the Pacific Northwest as well as the first person of color to hold a Seattle City Council seat.

I feel like a veil of racism has been lifted from Seattle politics.

What election has given you hope?

Is Law School Where I Belong?

It's my sophomore year in college. I'm beginning to think seriously about going to law school, but it seems so daunting.

First, there's the cost. I also have to have excellent grades. But the worst deterrent for me is that so many people seem skeptical.

Mom hosts a bridge party at our house. A woman in our neighborhood says to me, "You can't go to law school; you're a girl! If you go to law school, you'll lose your femininity."

I find this aggravating. Also strange.

Is femininity like virginity? Once it's gone, it's gone? I've already lost my virginity; what do I care about my femininity? It seems to me that femininity is what's keeping women in the kitchen. I want no part of that.

I know many lawyers from politics and the legislature, but I don't know any women who practice law. I have no role models; I don't feel like I belong.

Some of us aren't meant to belong. Some of us have to turn the world upside down and shake the hell out of it until we make our own place in it.
—Elizabeth Lowell

As If One of Our Own Has Been Taken

November 22, 1963. I walk into Condon Hall for a class. I stop in the ladies' room. Someone says that President Kennedy has been shot and killed. It must be a lie. When I get to class, the professor says school is closed. Now I know it's true.

Even though I wasn't twenty-one and old enough to vote, I worked hard on Kennedy's campaign, volunteering with the Democratic Central Committee. I'm devastated by his death.

Kennedy was dedicated to things that mattered. My parents and I valued his support for civil rights, equal education opportunities, and his commitment to overcoming poverty. His assassination inspires me to be a lawyer and to work for justice all the more. I crave some way, even if small, to make up for our loss.

Mom, Dad, and I gather in front of the TV for the whole of Thanksgiving. Despite the feast, it's a sorrowful time. Mom and Dad are patriotic. Dad puts the flag up every holiday. They vote at every opportunity and work to get others to vote. We share this loss as a family, as if one of our own has been taken.

Has a tragedy ever motivated you to do more?

3
CHAPTER THREE

What's the Worst That Could Happen?

When Good News Is Bad

Winter 1965. My third session at the Washington State Senate. I work on redistricting. No subject is more dear to the members of the legislature than this. It affects whether they will ever be elected again.

My work is winding down. I'm getting ready to leave Olympia. But something is wrong—very wrong.

I visit a doctor. "Yes, my dear," he says in a cheerful voice. "You are pregnant."

I'm horrified, but do not let my horror show. The thought occurs to me that he could pass on the fact that I'm unmarried to some agency that protects children. But he doesn't ask about the father. I pay for the visit in cash and get out of there as quickly as I can.

My shame is overwhelming.

How could I let my parents down like this? They've sacrificed so much in pursuit of the American Dream. They have a beautiful home, two cars, good jobs, and they secure a good education for each of their kids. Like many post-World War II parents, they work to make a life for my brothers and me that is free of the struggles they endured.

I have undone their American Dream. And ruined my own dream as well. I'll never become a lawyer.

I'm sure my parents will disown me when they find out. I brood for days. I know girls who've gotten pregnant with their boyfriends while still single. They have shotgun weddings. But those attending don't know about the shotgun.

Seven months later, they have a "premature" child, at full birth weight by some miracle. At least they aren't unwed mothers; the children have their father's name.

Mine will not. And I know what people will think. The Bridge Club women in our community consider being an unwed mother worse than committing a crime. And I thought I was going to be a lawyer.

I know some women have abortions. But abortions are illegal, so we never hear of those. The father of my child is married. There will be no wedding, shotgun or otherwise.

I've made my decision.

I'd rather take my life than put my parents through the humiliation of having a daughter who is an unwed mother.

I know the bus from Olympia travels up Route 99, stopping near the Aurora Bridge. From its highest point, 167 feet above the icy gray waters of Seattle's Lake Union, I'm certain no one has ever survived the jump.

Have you ever been so ashamed of something that you thought of suicide?

Where Am I Headed?

I'm at the Greyhound bus station in Olympia. I buy a ticket for Seattle and sit waiting, thinking. The bus doesn't stop near my home in Burien. It goes to downtown Seattle, where I have to catch another bus to White Center and then call to get a ride home.

Where is my life headed? I'm almost through college, but this pregnancy is upending everything.

On the bus, I look around. Is anyone else here thinking about suicide? The bus will stop close to the Aurora Bridge, Seattle's suicide destination. The very name Aurora conjures up pictures of pain, of jumpers and headlines, of emergency vehicles arriving too late, of police in boats searching for bodies.

Should I go south from Seattle to catch the bus home? To face my parents and face up to their disowning me? Or should I go north to face...?

Sometimes even to live is an act of courage.—Seneca

Sinner Seeks Strength

As I near the city limits, I remember that the Greyhound bus station is close to Seattle Unity, my church.

I started going to Seattle Unity after graduating from high school. I was unhappy with the Lutheran church I attended previously.

At my old church, they were always talking about sin. Suicide is a sin.

If I'm this bad, I ask myself, why bother? Dad, ever the optimist, says he can't wait to get to Heaven to see all the different rooms for Christianity, Islam, Hinduism, Buddhism, even Atheism.

A friend invited me to Seattle Unity. On my first visit, the minister spoke of "entering into prayer with all people everywhere, whether in a church, a temple, a mosque, or in nature." Here was a

Christian church without dogma; I'd found my home.

But now I *am* a sinner.

I will go to Seattle Unity. I will sit in the small round chapel. I will find the strength to do it.

Upon this rock, I will build my church; and the gates of hell shall not prevail against it.—Matthew 16:18

The Longest Twenty Minutes of My Life

It's dark and raining. I walk, my umbrella useless in the wind. I approach the church and try the door. It's locked, but I see lights inside. Sometimes they have evening meetings. I call from a phone booth to see if anyone's there.

I'm crying. The answering service gets Reverend O'Connor on the line. He says, "Whatever it is, sit tight. We'll be there in twenty minutes."

It's the longest twenty minutes of my life. I feel sick. I haven't eaten since breakfast but have no appetite. I close my umbrella and move in from the rain under the cover of the church eaves.

Soak up the views. Take in the bad weather and the good weather. You are not the storm.—Matt Haig

To Tell the Truth

I feel like a fool having the minister leave dinner to see me.

He and his wife pull up and unlock the doors to the church. I stifle my tears. Reverend O'Connor takes me into the small chapel. His wife gives me a hug and then leaves us alone.

Through tiny windows at the bottom of the chapel walls, I hear the patter of rain on the surface of the pond outside.

In a warm, majestic voice, Reverend O'Connor begins with prayer. After the prayer, he listens to my story. Pregnant with no father available, I tell him that I know my parents will disown me.

Should I tell him I'm thinking of suicide? If I do, will he call the police and have me taken to the hospital? No, he wouldn't do that.

I admit to him that I have thoughts of jumping off the Aurora Bridge. He takes my hands in his and tells me emphatically, "Your parents would never disown you."

He also tells me that no parent would want their child to commit suicide, that whenever a child commits suicide, the parents feel responsible, guilty that they have somehow failed. I don't want my parents to feel guilty when this is my own doing.

He convinces me to go home and tell the truth. I know he's right that my parents will be the ones to suffer most if I take my life. Still, I can't figure out how to tell Mom. She's such a perfect person. She won't understand how I could've gotten myself into this situation.

I walk to First Avenue to catch the bus to White Center, where I'll call Dad to pick me up and take me home.

What's the hardest thing you've ever had to do?

Family Secrets

Dad picks me up at the bus stop in Mom's shiny black 1965 Buick Riviera. He's in his usual good mood. He tells me he's missed me and cracks a few of his corny jokes.

He's not surprised that I don't laugh. His jokes generally meet with a groan. I don't tell him what I need to say. I have to tell Mom first.

Even though it's early evening, Mom's in bed. She has many chronic health problems, including a bad back.

As a realtor, Mom's on her feet all day, seven days a week, because of the open houses required. She works as many hours as it takes, not the predictable nine to five. And it's certainly not a desk job.

I dread laying this news on her when she's so ill. In the new expanded kitchen, our cockatiel, Tweety, is busy talking to our turtle, Snappy, in his fish tank next to her cage.

Dad offers me dinner. I can't eat. I head to Mom's bedroom in slow, weak steps.

Mom sits up as I enter. I sit next to her on the king-size bed. She reaches for a cigarette and offers me one. I decline. Then I begin.

"Mom, I don't know how to tell you this, but I'm pregnant."

She looks shocked but not outraged, as I would've expected. She even seems to smile a little.

"Who's the father?" she asks.

I expected this would be her first question, if not, "When's the wedding?"

I admit my shame to Mom: the father is a married man; it was a one-time thing between us; he doesn't know about it.

"Do you think you're the only one?" she says.

I'm confused.

"Your father is not Pat's father."

I don't know how to react.

Sitting up slightly, she explains that she got pregnant when she was twenty and living in Blair, Nebraska. She married her boyfriend because they "had to" get married. They quickly divorced after my brother's birth.

Dad came along shortly thereafter. He wanted to marry her and become Pat's father. He wanted Pat to know that he loved him as if Pat were his own.

Pat doesn't know he has another father. But I do. Now.

Bad news isn't wine. It doesn't improve with age.—Colin Powell

4
CHAPTER FOUR

In a Family Way

My Choice

How could I have ever thought my parents would disown me? What's the most important lesson I've been taught growing up? "Family first." My parents are willing to help me in any way they can.

Over the next week, we discuss options.

Abortion is illegal, but my mother knows a reputable doctor willing to do it. Or I can keep my baby, and my parents will help support us. Or they'll adopt my baby and raise it as their own child. Finally, I can choose a home for unwed mothers, have my baby there, and give it up for adoption.

I choose to give my baby up for adoption. It's my way of earning redemption by bringing joy into the lives of a family who perhaps can't have a child of their own.

I'll bear my loss as a secret shared only with my parents.

If we share our story with someone who responds with empathy and understanding, shame can't survive.—Brené Brown

There's No Place Like a Home Away from Home

As my parents and I plan for my baby, I wrestle with mixed feelings about motherhood. I notice, too, that my parents have feelings as mixed as mine about being grandparents.

They have two infant grandkids already by my older brother Tim. Unfortunately, their relationship with his wife is a bit off, so they don't get to see them as often as they'd like.

I think Mom wants my child to be born as much as I do, but not for the same reasons. Nonetheless, she respects my choice, and we begin to look for a place I can go to keep my pregnancy private.

Mom and I visit the Florence Crittenton Home, a home for unwed mothers in Seattle. Most of the girls here are teenagers, but I'm an adult. This difference brings up many uncomfortable feelings for me.

I realize I don't even want to be in Seattle right now and be seen pregnant. People will want to know who the father is and how a smart and ambitious young woman like me let something like this happen. I'll never outrun the rumors.

Apparently, there's another Florence Crittenton Home in Colorado, near Denver. This seems like the best solution. It's going to be expensive, but Mom and Dad are willing to do anything for me.

I tell my friends I'm going to Colorado to study the legislature there for my senior paper in political science and then over to Nebraska to visit relatives.

Who in your life has been willing to do anything for you?

Pretending to Be Someone I'm Not

March 1965. My first plane ride. If I weren't so ashamed and embarrassed about being pregnant, this might be exciting. When the plane takes off, I feel the surge of power. It's a rush! I instantly love flying.

I'll stay at the YWCA in Denver for several weeks to save money. Then, as I get close to my delivery date, I'll move to the Crittenton Home until the baby is born.

In high school, we read *The Scarlet Letter*. I feel like I'm wearing a big red letter "A" on my forehead even though no one knows that I'm single.

I feel like a failure but find the courage to make appointments with legislators and staff at the Colorado General Assembly.

Entering the general assembly, I wear a red suit with a pleated skirt and box jacket. I'm sure that I "show," but I'm wearing Mom's first wedding ring. No one asks embarrassing questions.

My three years working in the Washington State Legislature have prepared me well. The interviews are not as hard as I thought they'd be.

Back at the YWCA, I spend my time reflecting on the interviews and drafting my paper comparing Washington and Colorado. Each state is divided by a mountain range into a wet, industrial side and a dry, agricultural side. There are many similarities in the politics and attitudes of the legislators as well: liberal on one side, conservative on the other. The work is interesting, but I'm so lonely here.

Have you ever pretended to be someone you're not?

The Encouragement I Need

In May, I receive a letter from Wing Luke. He continues to encourage me to apply for law school and thinks I have a good chance of getting in.

He tells me that the University of Washington had thirty-four students in its first law school class in 1899, including one African American, one Japanese student, and three women. Still, I've heard rumors that the university now has a 12 percent quota on women.

What if they find out I've been an unwed mother? If I were a guy, no one would ask about children. But it's common for women to be asked in job interviews if they have or plan to have children. A law school interview might be the same.

Secrecy is essential. Still, based on Wing's encouragement, I plan to apply to the University of Washington.

Exploring the unknown requires tolerating uncertainty.
—Brian Greene

Making Friends in a Strange Place

I visit the Crittenton Home, where I'll be moving in soon. I look forward to seeing other people in my situation, even though most of them will be much younger.

I meet Cindy and Sue, who are also in college. We have a lot in common. We're from upper-middle-class families, and our parents know about our situation.

Cindy, Sue, and I form a bond. We spend time talking about how we got into this predicament. About the jerks who are the fathers. About what our parents think. About where we go from here.

I feel relieved from the loneliness of the past few months and optimistic about the future. We'll each make it through this together and go on to live good lives.

We're all studying something here. It helps pass the time, which is agonizingly slow when you're pregnant and don't want to be. I'm taking a typing class to improve my speed. Some of the guys I know in law school say typing is a real help. Despite all the barriers, I'm more determined than ever to become a lawyer.

Who is the friend you met in a strange place?

A Series of Continuous Progressive Contractions

The time is getting close now. I need to decide whether to have my baby in the delivery ward at Crittenton or go to the hospital.

My baby's health is priority number one. I think I should go to the hospital in case there are complications. It will cost more, so I'm calling Mom and Dad to see what they think.

I talk to some of the girls here who've recently delivered about what labor is like. I've been a babysitter for several women who had babies in our neighborhood. None of them ever talked about the pain of labor. So I look it up: Labor is a series of continuous progressive contractions of the uterus that help the cervix dilate. There's strong cramping in the abdomen, groin, and back, and for some in their sides or thighs as well.

There's a secret in our culture, and it's not that birth is painful. It's that women are strong.—Laura Stavoe

This Can't Be Happening!

Mom calls today because she doesn't want me to find out from the papers that Wing Luke is missing.

Wing and a friend went fishing in Eastern Washington with another friend who owns a private plane. The pilot filed a flight plan, but the weather turned bad, and they haven't been heard from.

Rescue planes are out looking.

When did you hold your breath in the face of unsettling news?

Alone, Angry, and in Pain

June 26, 1965. I'm starting to have contractions. I'm at the hospital in a room by myself. It's cold in here even though it's the end of June.

I'm writing a letter to my baby's father. I haven't told him about my pregnancy. He's married. I probably won't send this letter, but it gives me a chance to say, if only to myself, how angry I am.

I'm sure suspicions are that I've been knocked up by a legislator. That's not true. The father and I were classmates and friends in college. He's a television news reporter for the most popular TV station in Seattle. I often saw him on television as well as at school. We talked a lot about politics.

I knew he was married, but he was a bit of a celebrity, and I guess I was starstruck. A lunch became a motel visit and, soon after that, a baby. He hasn't contacted me since. How stupid could I be?

I wish I'd stayed at the Crittenton Home for delivery. It's the middle of the night, and I'm bawling and screaming, making way too much noise. There's no one down at this end of the hall, but I'm sure it annoys the nurses. They check on me every hour or so, but it's just a quick look, no conversation.

What was the worst night of your life?

Caught in the Undertow

I was told that giving birth would feel like bad menstrual cramps, but it's much more intense, almost all in my lower back.

Every time a contraction comes, my lower back seizes up. The muscles inside twist harder and harder until the pain is almost unbearable. Then it slowly subsides.

I'm very scared now. I feel like I'm caught in the undertow of a wave. I try to relax, but my water just broke, and the contractions are worse. I feel like someone's wringing my insides out like a wet dishrag. A nurse tells me she's calling the doctor for an epidural.

To live is to suffer, to survive is to find some meaning in the suffering.
—Friedrich Nietzsche

It's a Girl, But Not Mine

I have a girl. I give her a name, but I know it won't be her real name. It's the female version of her father's first name.

I checked into Crittenton under a fake name, too. If anyone tries to check up on me, they'll never know I was here.

Everyone says the baby is pretty. I don't want to look at her or hold her, but I need to, for her sake, so she'll feel secure.

I breathe her in. She smells delicious, like all new babies. I think of other tiny babies I've handled when babysitting.

My brother Tim has two infants, and my brother Pat's wife is due to deliver soon. Our whole family will soon celebrate Pat's child, but we won't celebrate mine.

Have you ever had something you wanted and didn't want
at the same time?

If Only I Had Used "The Pill"

I just talked to Mom. She's wrapping up a sale, and then she'll drive down here. She should arrive in four days, but it will take several more to get the adoption hearing.

My baby stays in the nursery here at the Crittenton Home. I check on her to change her diapers and bottle-feed her. I'm not breastfeeding, so she has the bottle from the beginning.

I'm leaking like a sieve. I want to get it stopped as soon as possible so no one in Seattle sees it.

If only I'd started taking "the pill" when it was first available, I wouldn't be here. But I'll start now. They say taking it helps to end lactation.

If only… The saddest words in the English language.—Kristan Higgins

I Won't Change My Mind

July 3. Mom's excited to see the baby. She says we'll talk about the final decision when she gets here, but I know I won't change my mind.

Nothing has changed for me about what I think is best for us both. If I kept her she would be stigmatized as a "bastard," and the future I have planned for myself would be impossible. Also, I don't want to disappoint the people who've been chosen to adopt her.

The caseworker describes them as kind, intelligent, and loving.

This will be their third adopted child. Other than that, I don't know anything about them. They won't know anything about me either, except the health history I provide.

May your choices reflect your hopes, not your fears. —Nelson Mandela

Or So He Says

I feel sick, and I'm bawling again. I call the father to tell him what's happened and to get the health information I need. He sounds sympathetic and asks what he can do. I wonder if he even believes it's his.

After talking to me for less than five minutes, he says he has to get off the phone because of a program deadline. He needs to film people trying to capture a lone whale in Puget Sound to send to a California zoo.

Or so he says.

I tear up all the drivel I wrote when I was in labor. It was so bitter and angry. I don't want anything from him now, especially not his sympathy.

Pain is certain, suffering is optional. —Buddha

This Isn't My Baby Anymore

Mom and I see the judge in an anteroom with no spectators. The caseworker explains the procedure one more time, and the judge repeats it.

Everyone wants to make sure I know what I'm doing, but I'm an educated adult, not a twelve-year-old. I just want the whole thing to be over.

I sign the papers. The judge takes the file and leaves the room. I hand my baby to the caseworker.

Mom asks me one more time if I want to have a photo. I tell her again that I don't. This isn't my baby anymore.

A part of me has departed with you.—Unknown

5
CHAPTER FIVE

Is Law School Still Possible?

What Comes Next for Me?

Fall 1965. I can complete my remaining degree credits by correspondence while I work. Meanwhile, Mom takes on one of the first condominium townhouse developments in Seattle. Due to a Boeing recession and cost overruns, units aren't selling. The developer thought they would be snatched up by Californians moving to Seattle.

Mom's been hired to turn things around. She disagrees about who will buy these homes. She believes the people who will buy them live close by. They're people who want to downsize and who will have homes of their own to sell.

Mom's marketing plan actually includes *raising* the prices. She wants better rockeries and more elaborate landscaping. She also wants more advertising: a full-size billboard within a few blocks of the development.

"If we devote ourselves to nothing but selling for the next year," she says, "we can sell these twenty homes." If she's right, I'll be able to go to law school.

In a few short weeks, I sell my first house all on my own. I feel a sense of accomplishment. I'm also starting to live up to Mom.

All that matters is what you do next.—Hrishikesh Agnihotri

The Search and the Sadness

May 1966. Even after a year, weekend private pilots still search for Wing Luke's plane.

During his life, newspapers featured him talking about the need to preserve the history of immigration of Asian Americans. Many artifacts of migration were lost in assimilation.

A small group of people, which my parents and I join, starts working on the idea of a memorial to Wing. Warren Chan, our first Asian American superior court judge and a close friend of Wing, is promoting the idea of an Asian American museum to fulfill the need Wing identified.

Our group includes people in law, education, journalism, the arts, architecture, real estate, the building trades, restaurants, and more. We're an enthusiastic little band, but we're unfunded and unskilled when it comes to building museums.

Wing was a good friend of the director of the Burke Museum at the University of Washington. The director offers to help us with the museum's design. Unfortunately, we learn that he's moving on to another museum in the East. We keep plugging away to see what we can accomplish.

Life is what you celebrate. All of it. Even its end.—Joanne Harris

Living by Choice, Not by Chance

I get a letter wait-listing me for the fall of 1966 at the University of Washington School of Law. My friend Richard, whose grades are similar to mine, gets accepted. Maybe the rumor about a quota for women is true.

Then I get accepted to Willamette University College of Law in Oregon. A friend at Willamette tells me that only one woman has been accepted there in the last eight years.

I know I should wait for word from the University of Washington because it would be less expensive, and I could live at home. But if I wait, Willamette may fill its class. So Willamette it will be!

When there's a maybe and a for sure, which would you rather have?

Sneaking Out of Town Once Again

August 1966. I'm excited about starting law school, but I don't tell many friends. I'm keeping quiet in case I don't make it. I'm sneaking out of town again but for a different reason this time. If I flunk out, I'll just sneak back.

Mom comes to Salem with me to look over the law school and help me choose a place to live. There are no campus living quarters for older female students.

As a temporary arrangement, I'm living at the historic Marion Hotel. I have a room with a four-poster bed, a bath, and an antique writing table. For meals, I eat at a nearby (male-only) boarding house that offers good home cooking. I'll have to watch my weight.

The dean at Willamette is a retired military officer who's willing to take a chance on a few women in our class. We would have been the first class in the $1.1 million Truman Wesley Collins Law School but construction is behind.

Our very large group, intended to occupy the new building, is crammed into Gatke Hall. Until 1938, it was a US post office. Then, it was rolled up on logs from downtown Salem to the campus. We also have some of our classes in the attic of a nearby building.

After working three terms at the Washington State Senate, I'm accustomed to being around so many men. There are no female professors here. There are a few female staff members, though I seldom see them because they're upstairs.

Today I talk to Phyllis, the dean's secretary. I mention how inconvenient it is to have to go across the street from campus to the Oregon Supreme Court to use the ladies' room.

Phyllis laughs and says, "Don't you know where the ladies' room is?"

"Is there one in the building?" I ask.

"Let me show you."

As we open the door to the library, about fifty male students look up.

Phyllis whispers, "Make a quick right at the first stack."

When I get to the end of the stack and turn right, indeed there's a door marked, "Ladies."

I open the door and have to turn myself sideways to enter. It's tiny, but it's better than crossing the busy street. There's a clock over the library entry door; the guys start timing my stay in the loo.

Being in law school with so few women makes me feel conspicuous. Everything I do is noticed, judged, and commented upon. Guys walking up the stairs behind me exchange comments intended for me to hear. They talk about how short my skirt is or isn't and whether my butt is too big or too small.

I feel simultaneously conspicuous and invisible. Like an oddity whom everyone notices but chooses to ignore.—Cristina Henríquez

First Year, They Scare You to Death

There's a saying about law school: the first year, they scare you to death; the second year, they work you to death; and the third year, they bore you to death.

My favorite class is Property Law because of my background in real estate and because the instructor is brilliant, droll, and always challenging. However, the first-year load is intimidating.

Some students use crib notes from upperclassmen. Some purchase outlines, such as "Gilbert's on Contracts." I'm afraid to take shortcuts. I attempt to read all the cases and do my own outlines.

I'm falling behind. I live in terror of being called on. I might be asked to recite the facts, holding, and legal reasoning of a case I haven't read yet.

Do you ever suffer from Lone Ranger syndrome?

Here for a Husband? You're Kidding

During these first three weeks, I spend time answering the same questions from my male colleagues over and over. One or two at a time, they approach me, usually in the library. They want to know why I've come to law school.

I begin to realize I'm supposed to have a lofty, even altruistic, reason for being here. The subtext is, "What are you doing here taking up a perfectly good draft deferment? Everyone knows you'll never practice law a day in your life. You're really here for an MRS degree, aren't you?"

I let it go for a couple of weeks, but it's demoralizing and interrupts my concentration.

It occurs to me to ask *them* what *they're* doing here. When I do, the answers aren't lofty or altruistic at all. Often I hear, "My father's a lawyer; it's expected of me." Or "What else can you do with a degree in history?" More often, it's "To make a lot of money."

Many of the students here have been undergrads living on campus in a very sheltered environment. Others are more worldly, but in some ways, this seems like going back to high school.

Of the four women who start law school this year, two are from Stockton, California. Both have perms. This hair fashion hasn't made it to Oregon yet, so "they must be lesbians." The guys call them Frizzy One and Frizzy Two or Lizzie One and Lizzie Two, all within earshot of these kind women. Now I hear they've left school even before first-semester exams.

I feel bad that I haven't stuck up for them. I guess I'm too busy sticking up for myself. The teasing I receive is juvenile, tedious, and exasperating. With finals coming up and my nerves on edge, one of my classmates reduces me to tears in the law library. Never shy, I'm ready to start dishing it back.

Have you ever felt like the odd one out?

The Lighter Side of Law School

Phyllis comes rushing up to me with big news: "The new law school is going to have a six-holer for its ladies' room!"

The other woman left in my class is Carol Beatty, a petite redhead with hair down to her waist and cornflower-blue eyes. By my count, at least half a dozen of my classmates are in love with her. She and I aren't close. If we stop in the hall to talk, the guys want to know what the conspiracy is.

Oddly, it's fine for me to talk with Bonnie Bailey, the woman in the class ahead of us. She's willowy and, like me, Irish, with dark brown hair and clear blue eyes. She's sweet, a great cook, a mentor, and a booster. She's invited me to room with her in her apartment second semester. Bonnie mothers the men in her class and me as well. I don't know how many of her classmates are in love with her, but at least three of mine are.

Bonnie and I occasionally throw an impromptu "study party" dinner at her apartment. We get everyone's money, mostly loose change. She and I go down to the meat market, where we cajole the butcher for several pounds of meat. We send everyone to their apartments to bring back whatever they can find: a few potatoes, a three-day-old head of lettuce, some bacon, etc. We then make it all into a sumptuous repast. Once in a while, someone brings Kahlúa, and someone else brings ice cream. When that happens, it's Kahlúa shakes for dessert.

A few students live in their family homes nearby, while most of us find apartments. One of our classmates is Rex Anthony Bell Jr. He's a little older and a lot richer than most of us.

Rex is from Las Vegas. He owns a clothing store and a few other enterprises there. His father, a cowboy movie star, is Rex Bell, a former lieutenant governor of Nevada. His mother is Clara Bow, the "It girl" of silent movies.

Rex has built his own house, which becomes a refuge for the few upscale law school parties we have.

The sight of women talking together has always made men uneasy; nowadays, it means rank subversion.—Germaine Greer

Am I the One Out of Three?

When I start law school, some professors remind us they're "throwing pearls before swine." Others say, "Look to the person on your left and right: one of you three is not going to make it." We're assigned our seating alphabetically. I look at Doug on my left and John on my right. We're in the second row, right under the instructor's nose.

I keep my grades to myself. I'm sure I'm down there at the bottom somewhere. Some of my classmates have been warned or asked to leave. So far, I haven't. Apparently, it's true that out of the 125 of us who begin, one-third will not graduate. Some say this is deliberate because law schools make their money on the L-1s and reduce the need for faculty for the L-3s.

Have you ever seen the movie The Paper Chase?
It's Harvard, of course, but it's not far off.

Is the Wing Luke Museum Just a Dream?

Late fall 1966. I continue to work in real estate during the summers and keep up with Wing Luke museum activities. My mother calls me in Oregon to tell me the group has decided the museum project is not doable. I ask her to call another meeting for a time I can attend. At the meeting, I make a pitch to everyone that we can and will do it.

We get our first grant. Harriet Rice of the Bullitt family makes it happen. It's $2,000, a fortune for us compared to what we've been working with. I drive back to Salem confident that Wing's dream will happen.

It's now two years since Wing's plane went missing. We lease a small storefront at 8th and King Street in Chinatown. Ben Woo, a talented architect, creates the logo and design. My father handles the plumbing and pounds nails with Ben. Betty Luke, Wing's younger sister, leads the curation efforts.

We collect and preserve artifacts of the Asian American immigrant experience, many dating back to the 19th century. One of our first exhibits is a giant folded paper display with workshops on how to create origami.

I keep the meetings and communications going, plan fundraisers and publicity, and even work on construction. We're all in Chinatown at all hours of the day and night, often grabbing dinner at Tai Tung after midnight. I begin to think of Chinatown as home.

It always seems impossible until it's done.—Nelson Mandela

Ruby Chow, Grande Dame of Chinatown

Ruby Chow was born in 1920 on a fishing pier in Seattle, where her family lived. Her father managed the San Juan Fishing and Canning Company. He immigrated as part of the labor force that built America's western railroads.

Ruby's father died in 1932, leaving her mother and seven children to fend for themselves during the Great Depression. Ruby was the oldest when her father died. She learned to run things when she was twelve.

Ruby Chow married Chinese opera star Ping Chow, and they created a restaurant where Ping cooked authentic Chinese feasts. Ruby entertained the Who's Who in Seattle, especially the press and politicians. My parents and I enjoyed those feasts, particularly at Chinese New Year.

When Warren Chan starts the Wing Luke museum, Ruby is right there. Warren's mother was one of the people who helped her family through the Depression. Ruby, Ping, and their many children are wonderful supporters of the museum.

A Chinese scholar, Mr. Loy Locke, keeps the museum open and gives tours to schoolchildren. We pay him next to nothing, but he faithfully serves the museum when he's not away in Vancouver, BC. There are rumors that he sometimes travels from there to his birthplace in mainland China.

Everywhere, immigrants have enriched and strengthened the fabric of American life.—President John F. Kennedy

What If?

The assassinations of Martin Luther King in April of 1968 and Robert F. Kennedy in June are demoralizing. It's hard to stay focused on school.

I'm nervous about starting second year. I have a criminal law professor who sometimes stutters, apologizes for his stuttering, and then assigns sixty pages of reading for the next day's class.

Law students thrive on "What if?" questions. We're studying criminal responsibility and the element of intent. A tall, lanky guy in our class, known to be glib, asks a question: "What if someone is standing on a volcano with a gun, and the volcano erupts, and the gun goes off, killing someone nearby?" This evokes a loud groan from our class. His question is unanimously voted worst "What if?" question of the year.

That class clown went on to become an outstanding Alaska legislator.

My Business Is Their Business Too

Fall 1968. I live a block from the law school, comforted by the sound and view of a stream outside my tiny second-story apartment. However, it seems that I'm always under surveillance. If a car with Washington plates parks near my apartment on the weekend, my classmates quiz me about the visitor, hoping for some juicy gossip.

I don't date classmates, although I do have quite an interest in an older student in the class behind me. He's from Pendleton, Oregon, and wears cowboy boots. Having lived in San Francisco for several years, he seems very sophisticated to me. But when I visit his apartment, I notice women's cosmetics in the bathroom. I suspect this crush is doomed.

Everybody's private business is public property.—Grandma Dowdel

A Prank and a Professional Possibility

It's third year. We don't sit alphabetically anymore. I sit in the back row, usually next to Ron Kurillo, who cracks jokes sotto voce. Soon, the professor reprimands the backbenchers and threatens to call on us.

I like most of my classes except tax class. Tax law scares me; it's all about numbers. There's definitely a direct correlation between my high level of fear and poor performance. I'm getting my worst grade in law school in that class.

One of our professors teaches Administrative Law. He's bright and engaging. His one oddity is the way that he pronounces superfluous, "super-flu-us," which seems to be a favorite word of his.

My friend Doug Dunham has a pool going. The idea is to see who can get called on and mispronounce superfluous the way the professor does. Of course, a dozen hands shoot up when he asks his first question that day. He calls on me, and I make the "correct" mispronunciation of superfluous, whereupon he says, "Well, that just goes to show that some people will do anything for money." Another classmate tipped him off to the prank. But I still win the pool, a tidy $1.65.

Bonnie Bailey is considering a legal writing career. She proposes that I go with her to San Francisco. There, we'll interview and test to become editors at Bancroft-Whitney, a prominent legal publisher. I would love to live in San Francisco, so I tag along.

Our morning at Bancroft-Whitney is pleasant if you don't count the testing. We lunch at the Franciscan and head back for a meeting with the personnel director. He describes the editing position but explains that we wouldn't be able to go into management because they have a policy that male professionals don't report to female professionals. No way will I work for a company with this policy.

A feminist is anyone who recognizes the equality and full humanity of women and men.—Gloria Steinem

6
CHAPTER SIX

Clearing the Bar

The Worry That Won't Go Away

Spring 1969. Even though it's more than six months away, I'm worried about the bar exam. In fact, I've been worried about it since before I went to law school. I know several smart young men who've flunked as many as five times.

Seventeen of us Willamette grads plan to take the Washington bar exam. To get ahead of the curve this spring, some of us are driving down to Eugene on Friday nights to the University of Oregon for the Oregon bar review course. Even though Oregon law differs from Washington law, I think the course will help.

Worry does not empty tomorrow of its sorrow; it empties today of its strength.—Corrie ten Boom

Let's All Get Married

There's quite a spate of marriages around graduation. One of my classmates, Ron Kurillo, a bit of a rogue, chivalrously (and platonically) squires me to these events. I think he appreciates not having to dig up a date. He's burned his bridges with many of the local ladies.

On a trip to Northeastern Oregon, we stop at his parents' house in Portland for lunch. Here I see another side of Ron, warm and respectful to his parents with no trace of sarcasm.

My classmate Carol Bailey is included in the wave of marriages. She's number three in the class and marrying Henry Hewitt, who is number one. They're getting married on graduation weekend. Number two is our class phantom, Paul Crampton, an Idaho farmer. He's only shown up to take exams. I wonder if he'll show up for graduation.

Which graduation do you remember best?

Suddenly...

My parents attend graduation, staying at the once-grand Marion Hotel, where I first lived in Salem. My cousin and his wife also come, bringing their truck to help move me back to Seattle.

My apartment is a shambles with most everything in boxes for the move home tomorrow. Graduation takes place on the campus football field. It's the first time I've been here.

I return to my apartment to finish the last of my packing. My doorbell rings. One of my most attractive classmates comes by with alcohol, probably intent on seducing me. I invite him in.

Soon, the doorbell rings again. When I say, "Who's there?" another of my classmates, perhaps with the same idea, answers.

In the final hours of my life as a female law student, I've suddenly become popular with the guys.

See You Later Alligator.—Bill Haley & His Comets

With a Little Help From My Friend

It's time to take the bar, so I check into a dorm on the University of Washington campus for the six-week bar review course. My roommate, Karen, greets me breezily. "Want a beer?" she offers. This would have been unheard of when I was in the dorms.

It's a co-ed dorm; no tedious man-sneaking required. The campus "skirts only" rule has also been eliminated. Women wear pants, jeans, even shorts; tie-dye is everywhere. This isn't the same university where I started college eight years ago.

We have three or four hours of class each day. I'm nauseous with fear most of the time. My mind chatters constantly as I compare myself to my quicker classmates. My eyes pass over the pages, but the material eludes me. Three pages later, I can't recall what I've read.

One of my favorite classmates, Paul Stritmatter, nicknamed "Strictmother" because he's the boss of us all, comes over the night before the exam and walks me around outside to calm me down.

I get by with a little help from my friends.—The Beatles

One Giant Leap

July 20, 1969. After the first day of the exam, some of the other dorm residents and I gather around the TV to watch the moon landing. In grainy images, we see astronaut Neil Armstrong stepping off the ladder of the Eagle landing craft. "That's one small step for man," he says. "One giant leap for mankind."

Everyone is elated. We're clearly ahead of the Russians now. But for me, the feeling is fleeting, overtaken by the knot in my stomach as I think about day two of the exam.

In every life, we have some trouble. But when you worry, you make it double. Don't worry, be happy.—Bobby McFerrin

Yet Another Gender Barrier

September 1969. Now that exams are over, I move back to my parents' house to sell residential real estate with Mom. She keeps zealous tabs on me, wanting to know where I'm going and what I'm doing every minute of the day or night.

It's true that residential realtors must always be on call. But it feels like an excuse to monitor who I'm with and what I'm doing. Now that I'm twenty-six years old, her hovering chafes. But I'm at her financial mercy, so I bite my tongue and avoid a declaration of independence.

I'm considering a career in commercial real estate. Mom started the South End residential office of Henry Broderick, the most established downtown real estate firm.

There are few women in commercial real estate. But my law degree might help me overcome the gender barrier.

Mom puts in a word with one of the vice presidents. He agrees to give me a try in the commercial department as its first woman.

On my first day at the downtown office, I have no desk, no phone, no prospect list, no territory, nor any training. I guess I'm expected to figure this out for myself.

They say opportunity knocks but once. We know that's not true.
Opportunity knocks all the time, but you have to be ready for it.
And it has to be ready for you.

Knowing Is Worse Than Waiting

I wake up every morning stewing about my bar exam results. I don't have a good feeling.

A friend calls to tell me he has just seen the passing list. My name isn't on it. I'm devastated. That's three years of my life down the drain.

I break the news to Mom, then go to my room to cry a large bucket of tears. I've let my parents down again.

A few days later, I head for the bar office. The day before, I got the official notice: I flunked. But after seeing my exam, I notice that I failed by only two points. I don't know if I feel better or worse. I was so close.

There's no challenge or appeal process. I can only wait until the winter exam and try again.

Failure is not the opposite of success, it's part of success.
—Arianna Huffington

Just Two More Points

Ron Kurillo passed the bar and has a job in the prosecutor's office. He comes to see me, bringing his three-inch-thick bar review outline. His instructions are simple: memorize everything highlighted in yellow; pay attention to the stuff highlighted in green, but don't memorize it; let the rest go. "Remember," he says, "you just need two more points."

When I'm not working, I study, but not as frantically this time. I say to myself every day: "I just need two more points."

Mom and Dad loan me the money to buy a car—a silver 1970 Datsun 2000 convertible. Driving to Salem for a classmate's wedding, I dread seeing everyone. They'll ask about the bar exam; I'll have to tell them I flunked.

At the wedding, guys gather around my car. Someone asks if I'm practicing law. I break the bad news. "Oh well," my friend Phil says. "You'll pass next time. Now, about this car..."

Why do the birds go on singing? Why do the stars glow above? Don't they know it's the end of the world?—Sharon Van Etten

I Need a New Affirmation

October 1969. With the exam a few months away, I'm brushing up on positive thinking. The first time I took the bar, I used a simple affirmation: "I will pass the Washington State Bar Exam." Obviously, that didn't work.

I learned about affirmations from Lou Tice, owner of the Pacific Institute, a motivation and leadership company. He was a teacher and football coach at my high school.

Lou teaches that an affirmation is a first-person, present-tense, positive statement of the objective as though it has already happened, coupled with a vivid picture that evokes a positive emotion.

I immediately see the flaws in my original affirmation. It wasn't in the present tense, and every time I said it and thought of the exam, I got shivers down my spine—not a positive emotion.

I create a new affirmation: "I am now a member of the Washington State Bar Association." When I say it, I see myself being sworn in. I'm wearing my favorite yellow A-line dress with the matching coat and yellow picture hat, standing in the presiding department at King County Superior Court, my right hand raised.

Stating this in the present tense, I have no trouble believing it. I also get a rush of pleasure from picturing myself being sworn in.

The five Ps of an effective affirmation are first person, present tense, positive statement, and the creation of a mental picture that evokes pleasure.

An Important Lesson

It's happening today.

I'm being sworn in after the February bar exam, along with thirty others. The presiding judge asks us to raise our hands to take the oath. Out of the corner of my eye, I see Mom and Dad looking on proudly.

Since flunking the bar, I've learned an important lesson. People don't love us for our achievements. They love us for who we are—because we're family, because we're kind, goofy, whatever—not because of our accomplishments.

Failure is another stepping stone to greatness.—Oprah Winfrey

7
CHAPTER SEVEN

The First of Many Firsts

Intolerable Interviews

April 1970. I'm looking for my first legal job in another of Seattle's major Boeing recessions. I call a firm advertising for a trial lawyer. The senior partner asks me if I think that, as a woman, I can "stand the rigors of trial practice."

I'm stopped cold. I don't know any women I can point to and say, "Of course, look at her." I'm sure there are female trial lawyers, but I haven't met them yet.

I can't imagine what the "rigors" are. It's not backbreaking work like digging ditches or loading trucks.

A senior partner at a prestigious firm agrees to interview me at the Rainier Club, one of Seattle's most elegant private clubs. There's never been a female member here, except for the wives of members. As a woman alone, I must enter by a side door.

The senior partner interviews me in the club library, where drinks are served. At one point, he puts his hand on my thigh. I cringe. The "interview" is creepy, meaningless, and insulting.

What's your best (or worst) job-hunting story?

Honest Lawyers, Two Flights Up

There's an ad in the bar news for trial work with a small firm in the University District. On University Way, which everyone calls "the Ave," I find the offices of McCune and Godfrey, just past a bank and a shoe shop on Northeast 45th.

I trudge up two flights of well-worn linoleum stairs. At the top is a warren of offices with old wooden floors. In some places, the carpet looks ancient. The furniture is a mismatch of nice antiques and thrift-store purchases. There's a venerable grubbiness to the place but little charm.

Calmar "Cal" McCune, the senior partner, interviews me. He's tall though somewhat stoop-shouldered, an imposing man with silver hair, bushy brows, and large ears. His voice is gruff, his manner firm yet gentle.

We share a love of real estate law, but I tell him I'm interested in the trial work he advertised. He explains that a former associate left for health reasons. There's a large stack of Safeco Insurance subrogation cases needing immediate attention.

McCune is a moderate Republican: mainstream, fiscally conservative, modern of thought, progressive of purpose, and tolerant. He likes that I'm a Democrat because he wants political balance in the firm. He asks me where I see myself in ten years. Before I answer, he says, "Never mind. You'll be in the judiciary." I'm surprised. I've never thought of being a judge.

If I'm hired, I won't be the first female lawyer at the firm. Cal tells me they had a legal secretary who went to law school, became a lawyer, and returned to the firm to practice. Later, she went back to law school to become a law librarian. They're very proud of her.

I think I might like it here.

A bend in the road is not the end of the road. Unless you fail to make the turn.—Helen Keller

The Fundamentals

I get the offer.

It's exciting to start right away with litigation. But other than my law degree and bar admission, I don't have any practical experience. I'm assured that the partners are available to me at any time. I only have to ask. Fiercely independent as I am, I probably won't ask much.

My boss, Cal McCune, is known as the "Mayor of the University District." During the UW campus and Ave riots the previous summer, he was everywhere: presiding at the University District Rotary Club, meeting with the Black Panthers, and also with the chief of police. He helped get life on the Ave back to normal.

I meet a legal secretary named Jane who I quickly realize is my real boss. She says she'll teach me the fundamentals of legal practice, like how to get to the courthouse and whether the pink copy or the gold copy goes to the clerk's office.

A new job is like a blank book, and you are the author.—Unknown

An Unexpected Friendship

Summer 1970. Mom has a listing on a home owned by the wife of Judge Warren Chan. The house is on Puget Sound, not far from where I live. She wants me to meet the tenant, a female probation officer. Mom's sure we'll hit it off.

We meet at the French bistro in the bowels of the Smith Tower near the pergola in Pioneer Square. Lucy is a pretty woman with soft brown hair and eyes to match. She has a confidence that goes with her newly minted MSW from the University of Washington.

We exchange war stories about our respective lives in a man's world. We gossip about lawyers and judges we know.

I tell Lucy about Ron Kurillo. He's been badgering me to find him a date because he's new in town.

"This guy's a rogue, the love 'em and leave 'em kind," I tell her. "But he's very funny and would probably be an entertaining date if you don't take him seriously."

Lucy says, "Most of the guys I meet are either criminals or married cops. So why not?"

I call Ron.

"I have a friend I'd like you to meet," I say. "But with all the single guys I know, I shouldn't squander her on you."

Ron swears he's reformed and says he'll be a perfect gentleman.

The three of us meet at a bar in front of the Lombardi building under a sign that says, "State Hotel Rooms 75¢." Ron, on his best behavior, buys cocktails and pan-fried oysters to share.

Predicting is very hard, particularly when it's about the future.
—Yogi Berra

John R.

My firm pays my tuition to attend the Washington State Bar Association meeting in Vancouver, BC. I wear a sleeveless black linen dress with white piping and a matching coat. My skirt is short, as is the fashion, but not outrageously so. I sit in the front row, so I don't miss a thing.

I'm attending a session called "How to Make Money Handling Wrongful Death Cases." The speaker is John R. "Jack" Lewis from Moses Lake, a small town in Eastern Washington.

John R. from Moses Lake is big, puppy-dog happy, and whip-smart. Most speakers say their subjects are highly complex, but not this guy. He makes every case sound simple.

I'm wondering how I can continue to learn from him. Then I notice he's checking out my legs from the speaker's podium.

He has a huge cart with folders of sample pleadings, legal digests, and how-to pointers for us to take home. He brought a hundred sets, but there are several hundred of us in attendance. John R.'s session is the hit of the conference.

As the program ends, I rush to grab one of the folders. I turn back and see him smiling at me. He introduces himself, as if that were necessary, and invites me to lunch. I tell him I'm planning to attend the bar luncheon. He makes a deprecating remark about the speaker but agrees to join me.

After lunch, I tell him I have a probate issue I'm concerned about. He says probate cases are simple; anyone can do them. Next time he's in Seattle, he says he'll take me to the courthouse and introduce me to Don Swanson, who works in the clerk's office. Even though Don isn't a lawyer, John R. says he's a master of probate law.

John R. must be at least 6' 2" and nearly three hundred pounds. Standing next to him, I feel like a toy. He quickly establishes that I'm single and tells me that he is too. He says marriage is a trap. He's been there twice, with one spoiled kid from each relationship to show for it.

Am I to be a protégé with benefits?

Never Reinvent the Wheel

A big shot in the Washington State Trial Lawyers Association, John R. comes to Seattle for their meetings. True to his word, he calls me for a tour of the courthouse. I've been there many times, but today it's a different place. We start halfway up, on the sixth floor, which is shared between the law library and the clerk's office.

John R. asks Don Swanson to make me a copy of several types of probate cases handled by the best probate lawyers in town. For each type of probate case, all the forms have been completed. I need only copy them, substituting the names and facts from *my* cases. "Never reinvent the wheel," John R. preaches. "Save your energy for the shit that matters, like legal research and handling juries."

Everyone here treats John R. like royalty. I wonder if there's anyone who doesn't know him.

He takes me to the presiding department on the ninth floor and waltzes me into the inner offices behind a glass door to see Bob

Rockman, "the most important guy in this shithouse."

After some witty and profane banter, John R. says, "I'm counting on you to take care of her, Rockman."

"Done," Rockman replies.

As we visit each part of the courthouse, John R. introduces me to the staff, librarians, clerks, guards, and a janitor or two. He knows almost everyone's name—or at least their preferred brand of liquor, which he distributes copiously at Christmas each year. For Rockman, it's Chivas Regal by the case.

Rockman is the administrative staff person in the presiding department. He decides which judges get which cases and which cases are assigned to which courtrooms.

When your case is set for trial, you appear at the presiding department. You hang around with thirty to fifty people, waiting for your case to be assigned. If you don't want to wait several days, you don't cross Rockman.

John R. is a fountain of practical legal training. I absorb as much as I can. My homework assignment is to curl up each night with the Washington Court Rules, a green-bound behemoth with all the rules for each court level and a summary of each significant case concerning the rule.

Make the Court Rules your best friend, or they will be your worst enemy.
    —John R.

Calling a Bluff

The first witness in my car crash case is a police officer who blurts out that he "ticketed the driver"—clearly inadmissible in a civil case. Defense counsel objects and asks for a mistrial. The jury is sent out. Defense counsel asks that the jury be dismissed and our case put back to the bottom of the calendar for assignment of a new trial date.

I invite defense counsel to show the rule that requires this. He's silent. I ask the judge to impanel a new jury immediately. The defense attorney doesn't even touch the rule book on his desk. I've called his bluff. The judge immediately orders a new jury, saving us a year of delay. I see John R.'s point about the Court Rules.

On a weekend, John R. comes to my "honest lawyers, two flights up" offices. He surveys the premises with a few derisive snorts, then says I must immediately buy my own books. He tells me which sets I need and that he'll have his Bancroft-Whitney guy call me. I can pay for my books in monthly installments.

"The state statutes should be no more than an arm's length away from your chair," says John R. "Nine out of ten legal questions can be answered in the statutes."

Then he says, "Booksellers spread your reputation in the legal community. Whether it's good or bad depends on how fast you pay your book bills. Make sure it's fast."

Today a reader, tomorrow a leader.—Margaret Fuller

I Wish They'd Called First

From my years working with lobbyists at the legislature, I'm used to being wined and dined by men spending lavishly. But John R. takes it to a new level.

He stays at the Washington Athletic Club, an elegant private facility in the heart of downtown Seattle. It's guarded by doormen and a concierge who checks membership cards—but not John R.'s; he knows every doorman down to his shoe size, and they know him.

He's a big tipper. He eats in only the finest restaurants: Canlis, El Gaucho, and Rosellini's 410. His typical fare is filet mignon or chateaubriand. He orders an entrée as an appetizer. When I start in on the edge of a steak, he tells me to cut into the center. "Always eat the best part first," he says.

My apartment is in a motel-style low-rise from the 1950s with an outside entrance a few blocks south of the Alki lighthouse. A few yards away, I can hear the waves splashing onto a gray sandy beach or crashing into a bulkhead.

One Saturday morning, my parents unexpectedly drop by while John R. and I are having coffee.

Mom appraises him critically.

He's sixteen years my senior. Strike one. He's commanding and not subject to motherly intimidation. Strike two. His suit jacket is carefully draped on a chair, suggesting he did not arrive this morning. Strike three.

I brace myself for the clash of wills I'll soon be dealing with.

Have you ever said, "To hell with what my parents think?"

Matchmaker?

Lucy and I meet up for lunch on a Saturday at Ivar's Acres of Clams, Seattle's famous seafood restaurant. She tells me about her work evaluating defendants for the court for the purposes of sentencing.

Federal judges have wide discretion in the range of sentences they can impose. Lucy can't discuss specific cases, but she talks about her process. I don't do much criminal work, so it's interesting to hear.

What I really want to hear, however, is how she and Ron Kurillo are getting on. She tells me they've been dating every week since they met, and she thinks it's getting serious.

I laugh. Ron, the rogue, serious?

Then I think of the Ron I saw at his parents' house: respectful, thoughtful, warm, caring. Maybe that's the Ron she's getting to know.

Matchmaker, matchmaker, make me a match. Find me a find, catch me a catch.—Fiddler on the Roof

The Man of Her Dreams

December 27, 1970. Lucy calls me in tears. The man of her dreams is dead.

Driving to Portland to visit his parents, Ron Kurillo was hit head-on by a drunk driver. I feel like I've lost a family member.

I think back to dinner with Ron's parents and what a gracious man he was. I think of what he accomplished professionally as a lawyer and a King County deputy prosecuting attorney. I think of the promise he made to me that with Lucy, he would be the perfect gentleman.

Lucy and Ron had known each other for less than six months. Yet their love had clearly blossomed.

I'll spend time with Lucy, helping her to grieve and yet go on. I'll make her the dear friend Ron was to me.

The greatest tribute we can give to the deceased is to keep on living. For when we don't, we too shall die before our time.—Charles Glassman

Wear Something Nice

Mom calls to remind me that there's a banquet tomorrow for the Chinese Community Service Organization. She wants me to meet her and Dad there. She asks if I can be there on time. I tell her I have a court matter, but I'm pretty sure I can make it. Oddly, she says, "Wear something nice."

At the banquet, I see many familiar faces from our work in Chinatown. When I was in high school, and the Chinese girls' drill team was in a parade, we came to help with the arrangements. Dad worked stringing the many red Chinese lanterns over the streets in Chinatown. Then, of course, there was the Wing Luke Museum, where I worked on our main fundraising event, the Wing Luke Art Auctions.

I often got to meet the artists and even choose which art pieces the auction would receive. Currently, I serve as its vice president.

Cheryl Chow, Ruby's youngest and only daughter, is the MC tonight. She's a public school teacher and a girls' basketball coach. She has her mother's outspoken leadership skills, but she's her own person with a sometimes wry sense of humor that keeps audiences on their toes.

As I'm biting into a Cantonese spring roll, I hear my name called.

Mom, sitting by my side, says, "Step up there." I approach the front of the room and am met by Ruby Chow, holding a box marked with Chinese symbols. Cheryl Chow announces to the audience that the Chinese Community Service Organization is presenting me with the Chinese Man of the Year award.

Ruby opens the box and unwraps a beautiful Chinese scroll. Cheryl lists my contributions meriting the award. This award has been presented to other non-Chinese people for work on behalf of the community but never to a woman. My cheeks flush red with surprise and embarrassment as Ruby and I take photos together.

What has been your favorite surprise?

8
CHAPTER EIGHT

New Friends, New Experiences

Apparently, I Need a New Apartment

January 1971. I wake up to loud noises and see huge flames. I dash forward and discover with relief that the fire isn't in my apartment. It's reflecting in my window from a newer apartment building next door. There's a good distance between us, but it's still scary.

When I tell John R. what happened, he tells me that my apartment doesn't suit me. As a single woman, he says, I should be in Madison Park where all the cool young people and wealthy older people live. He says he's taking me apartment shopping.

With the recession, nice apartments are plentiful and reasonably priced. I find a stunning end apartment built out over the calm waters of Lake Washington, with gentle waves lapping at the dock below and a commanding view of Bellevue, a posh Seattle suburb. John R. approves but says it will need new carpets, window treatments, paint, and furniture.

The landlord will pay for the painting and the carpets. Still, the rest takes my breath away; there's no way I can afford it. In his usual style, John R. says, "No problem!" Then he takes me to Seattle's premier interior design shop.

I ask him, "Am I to be a kept woman?" He makes a fat down payment. "Chicken feed," he says. "No strings attached."

Installment payments I can afford are set on the balance.

If there is only one thing in my life that I am proud of, it's that I've never been a kept woman.—Marilyn Monroe

Bowling? No! Golf? No! Skiing? Yes!

In college, I had to take two physical education courses. I chose bowling and golf because I only had to change my shoes and didn't have to sweat. John R. wants to help me with the only sport I've ever truly wanted to try: skiing.

Now that school expenses are behind me, I buy skis and take a few lessons on the slopes at nearby Snoqualmie Pass. John R. takes lessons with me, but he operates on a different scale, booking ten days in a Sun Valley, Idaho condo with a private instructor for the two of us.

In Sun Valley, John R. takes me shopping and insists on buying me a gorgeous orange ski outfit. I won't be able to hide in that! We struggle on the slopes but manage, for the most part, to stay upright and in control.

Off the slopes, John R. books the best restaurants for our stay. One night, it's the subdued Christiania dining room. He's his usual flamboyant, entertaining self. To the consternation of management, half the diners are alienated and leave; the other half join us. Among them are an executive at GM and a few other high fliers. They talk about skiing, cars, foreign exchange, and real estate. John R. invites them all to dine at our condo.

After the next day's skiing, John R. makes the rounds of all the best Sun Valley restaurants, picking up a couple of whole chickens for appetizers. He buys chili at Gretchen's. At Atkinsons' Market, he buys giant Idaho potatoes to bake. He has steak filets cut two inches thick.

At dinner, it's clear to me that lifelong friendships are being made. These high-powered men are sketching out future ski and business trips. The women with them talk little. I'm the youngest and busy myself with serving.

Skiing is the next best thing to having wings.—Oprah Winfrey

The Shy Girl Never Gets Laid

Trial lawyers are a different breed. They're brash, bold risk-takers. They talk about justice and civil rights with zeal while still harboring their generation's prejudices against women and minorities. John R. brings me into the trial lawyer fold.

Few, if any, women are active in the Washington State Trial Lawyers Association. Grudgingly accepted, I'm treated like John R.'s girlfriend. I'm useful, have political connections, and know how to get things done.

John R., the Trial Lawyers president, convinces the organization that they should be more modern and have a woman on the board. After much debate, they decide to amend their bylaws to allow for the position of "recording secretary"—for me. I'll be a non-voting member of the board, but I don't have to take notes. I'll also be the chair of the legislative committee.

I understand tokenism, but when I experience it, I grab the token. As John R. says, "The shy girl never gets laid."

The insurance industry is lobbying to get "no-fault" insurance passed. No-fault insurance has a nice sound to it. But in reality, it caps what an injured person (or survivors of someone who's killed) can receive in damages. Cleverly, the companies still retain the right to fight among themselves over who is at fault.

Despite my familiarity with the legislature, as chair of the legislative committee, I'm nervous. As a countermove, our committee proposes eliminating the draconian "contributory negligence" rule, which says that if an injured person is even a little bit at fault—even one percent—they can't recover damages from the driver who is more at fault.

Our bill is called the "comparative fault law." It would reduce damages (but not eliminate them) by whatever percentage the jury determines the plaintiff is at fault.

Having John R. with me at the legislature is both a comfort and a source of fear. Having run as a Republican for the US Senate, he knows all the people on the other side of the aisle. I know all the people on the Democratic side.

John R. is a bull of a man. As we go from majority leader to whip to judiciary chair, I fear he may smash a teacup. But he doesn't.

We defeat no-fault insurance. We're going to celebrate at our board meeting this morning. Even better, the governor has signed the comparative fault law bill. A new day for justice dawns in Washington state.

Justice will not be served until those who are unaffected are as outraged as those who are.—Benjamin Franklin

Marriage? Me?

Mike is a defense attorney who often represents the other side in my cases. He's also a regular at cocktail hour at McCormick's bar. He sits at the table where Lucy and I sit.

He starts complaining bitterly about the new comparative fault law. I remind him, "Hey, we've created a lot of new business for you. Cases that previously would not get to trial will be generating billable hours for you all the way to verdict. Besides," I add, "it's the insurance companies' money, not yours!" (John R. is rubbing off on me.)

Much to Mom's relief, my relationship with John R. fades into friendship. I think he liked me because he knew he had things for me that would change my life.

"When I think you're ready for marriage," he once told me, "I'll pick your husband." I laughed.

Is marriage a win for women these days? I'm able to earn a living sufficient to buy my own car and home and to make investments. What do I gain in marriage? Wouldn't it just amount to a man telling me what to do?

Don't confuse having a career with having a life.—Hillary Clinton

Let's Take a Run

Every winter Wednesday night, I head out for skiing at Snoqualmie Pass. Tonight, I'm graduating to the slopes of Alpental, which are more challenging. Better yet, Alpental has a decent bar and a classic Bavarian chalet that offers a beautiful view up the slope where I marvel at a kaleidoscope of ski suit colors worn by awful-to-awesome skiers on groomed, white runs.

It's cold, and I'm alone tonight. As I stand by a fire with hot cider, I notice a kid in his early twenties looking my direction. He's short and slender with shoulder-length curly hair that gives him a girlish look until I notice the buff body and mustache. I look behind me to see who he's staring at. There's only the fireplace.

I head downstairs to a pay phone to make a call. As I'm dropping in dimes, I see the guy walk past me. He winks. This time, I don't look behind me.

Back upstairs, Charley introduces himself. His voice is cool and languid.

"Let's take a run," he says.

"I'm just a beginner," I say, begging off.

"I'll teach you."

He's like liquid on the slopes. But he stops frequently for me to catch up.

It turns out he's a former ski racer from White Pass, a rugged, no-frills ski area twelve miles southeast of Mount Ranier. At White Pass, he skis with the Mahre twins, Phil and Steve, when the two of them aren't training with the US Ski Team.

He blows me some smoke about how my skiing isn't that bad.

With new equipment and more instruction, he thinks I can become a good skier. I figure he's thinking I can become a mediocre skier. He's patronizing me. And he's nearly a decade younger.

Generally, I'm into older men, but somehow, I let this guy hang with me.

He offers to take me shopping for new equipment. He picks out new boots for me to try on and this year's hottest skis: K2s, made on Vashon Island, just across Puget Sound. "It's what Phil and Steve Mahre ski on," he says.

Who are your sports heroes?

Going Solo

Working at McCune and Godfrey, I have the opportunity to take nearly every kind of case at least once. I have a bankruptcy, a few probates, and lots of insurance cases, car crashes, slip-and-falls, boundary disputes, and business litigation.

But after three years with this firm in the University District, I'd rather practice downtown. As a trial lawyer, I want to be close to the courthouse. I also want a more attractive office.

Pioneer Square, just blocks from the courthouse, is undergoing major renovations. Two lawyers who took the bar about the same time I did want me to join them in a partnership. I like them, but I don't know much about their practices or their ethics.

In this buyer's real estate market, they're as busy buying properties as they are practicing law. I decide that sharing offices would suit me better, so we're signing a lease in a historic, completely renovated building known as Grand Central on the Park.

At Antique Liquidators, a huge warehouse full of early American pieces and other items, I buy a loveseat and rocking chair for our small lobby and a conference room table. Dad has an antique plow that R. David Adams, a talented floral designer in our building, mounts for me over the room divider between the reception area and offices with a miniature field of tall grasses around it. I have an antique table for client meetings and a rolltop desk.

Today, I'm having a grand opening. Former colleagues, clients, friends from the Wing Luke museum, judges, and lawyers stop by for cocktails and snacks. My friend Ben Woo brings an amaryllis with red-orange flowers. He promises I won't be able to kill it, even with my black thumb.

I worry about having enough business, but the phone rings constantly. I get referrals from lawyers who don't do family law cases or who have an "impossible" personal injury case to send my way.

When have you started what others thought impossible?

Is This for Twelve-Year-Olds?

Ski season has ended at Alpental, but Charley drops by with some ski-racing newspapers. He tells me to go through the back pages and pick out the ski camp I'm going to attend this summer. I laugh to humor him. Ski camp sounds like it's for twelve-year-olds.

He takes the paper and circles a couple of adult camps, one at

Palisades Tahoe in California and one in Grand Targhee, Wyoming. "This is crazy," I tell him. But I check my trial schedule. Targhee in June works.

When I mention to Mom that I'm going skiing in a few weeks, she takes a dramatic breath. "How can you do that?" she exclaims. "You shouldn't even think about a vacation until you have six months of overhead in the bank." Given my propensity to take risky or even hopeless cases, I wonder if I'll *ever* have six months of overhead in the bank.

Have you ever been glad you didn't let being an adult stop you?

Never Closer to God

Getting to Targhee means flying into Boise, followed by a thrilling small plane ride into Idaho Falls. From there, a green and white van takes us uphill from the secluded Teton Valley. It's two hours of magic: early summer dappled alpine views and scenic but scary overlooks. I can't imagine there's actually snow up there somewhere. I arrive still worried about how I'll fit in as an over-thirty beginning skier.

Today starts early with a hearty breakfast and some stretches so we can be on the slopes by 8 a.m. I'm the oldest skier here, but at least everyone's an adult. The coaches are world-class skiers picking up pocket money for the summer.

I ride up in the chair alone. This becomes my morning meditation. I'm never closer to God than when I'm on a ski chair. It's so quiet. In the distance, I hear a creek rushing. The air is crisp and clean. I'm anxious but mostly excited.

We learn the laws of downhill skiing physics. Skier stance: ankles, knees, and hips bent, shoulders forward, chest up, and squared down the hill. We drill skier safety (poles tucked) and chair etiquette. "Toes up" is a trick to get us to flex our ankles, thereby defying gravity and keeping us off our butts.

The week goes by in a flash.

You don't learn to walk by following rules. You learn by doing and by falling over.—Sir Richard Branson

The First Successful Female Commercial Realtor

I attend a reunion of the Henry Broderick gang. The old commercial real estate crew is a fun, successful, competitive group of men.

While I was in law school and commuting frequently from Salem to Seattle, I saw their work transform the Duwamish and Kent Valleys from farmlands to office parks, warehouses, and shopping malls. They made a lot of money. Still, I was relieved to say goodbye to them and go to work as a lawyer.

The Broderick firm was long viewed as *the* commercial firm in Seattle. It's now merged with a national company to become Broderick Coldwell Banker. Several guys compliment me on my success as a lawyer and say they always knew I could do it.

One of them tells me, "There's another woman who claims to be the first female commercial realtor at the firm. But we know it isn't true; you were." I reply, "Let's just say she's the firm's first successful female commercial realtor."

They confess to pulling some pranks on me when I was there, such as tearing up my phone messages. They expect me to think it's funny too. I smile, but I don't laugh.

Still in recession in 1971, Boeing has laid off 50 percent of its workforce due to the loss of the SST or supersonic transport as it's called. My Broderick pals, these same guys who got rich in commercial real estate, have paid for a billboard that reads: "Will the last person leaving Seattle please turn out the lights."

Have you ever been glad you didn't succeed?

9
CHAPTER NINE

Kim

My Kind of Girlfriend

Spring 1972. I enter the elevator with two other young women. One says, "Did you see that girl lying topless on our dock?" They're aghast. I'm wondering who this girl is and thinking I should meet her.

Pulling into my garage today, I notice a young woman in a red Corvette convertible. We chat about the 'Vette. "It belongs to a friend," she tells me. "I pick up mine tomorrow, which is just like it, only silver."

A periodontist, she's moved here from Boston to teach at the University of Washington dental school. Something about her boldness tells me she's the topless one.

"Kim Haglund," she says, with a firm handshake. I ask her if she's related to Ivar Haglund, founder of Ivar's Acres of Clams. "No," she says. "But this comes up so often, I think I'm going to ask him to adopt me."

Kim's buying her Corvette from my friend Terry Skiple at University Chevrolet. Terry sold me the black Chevy Impala I drive.

Kim gives Terry the nickname Skippy, and the three of us become fast friends, meeting for lunch or cocktails at Seattle's trendiest restaurants—as long as they have great salads. Kim's a budding vegetarian.

A true Scandinavian blonde with mischievous blue eyes, at 5' 2" and scarcely a hundred pounds, Kim looks like a miniature Jane Fonda. She's the woman miniskirts were invented for and usually wears them with tall suede or leather boots. She swears like a truck driver—literally—a habit learned in her summers driving a dynamite truck for road crews in Ontario, Canada, to put herself through dental school.

It was Terry who drove her around the city and said she needed to live in Madison Park. He told her it's the neighborhood for affluent singles, tennis nuts, and well-off families.

She settles for a studio because her first choice, Anchors East, has a waiting list. After the Corvette, her next purchase is a Doberman Pinscher puppy she names Rommel. He loves riding in the 'Vette with his head and bandaged cropped ears in the wind. The back seat is his domain.

All for one and one for all.—Alexandre Dumas

Like a Pied Piper

There's an energy about Kim that swoops people into her vortex.

We're waiting for a table at Latitude 47. She strikes up a conversation with an old guy with ratty clothes, straight brown hair that looks like it hasn't been cut for a decade, and awful teeth.

It turns out he owns several junk shops. He specializes in unwanted properties in down markets. Migrating from Ballard to Rainier Valley, he's acquired a large commercial property his son will use for a junk car business.

He's a patient of Kim's in fifteen minutes. He'll soon be getting gum surgery and then a referral to one of her colleagues for a complete mouth restoration. He looks like he hasn't spent five dollars on himself in the last year. I wonder if he knows he's just committed to thousands in dental work.

Even though he's probably thirty years Kim's senior, he's clearly smitten with her. He wants to know when we can meet for drinks.

Like a pied piper, Kim makes friends fast. Women enjoy her warmth; men melt in her effervescent smile and perfect white teeth. "If you've got 'em, floss 'em," she quips.

Kim and I talk incessantly about our careers. We're both highly conspicuous in our professions. There are few female dentists in Seattle, let alone periodontists. She's as passionate about her work as I am about mine.

In addition to managing her University of Washington class and clinic schedule, Kim quickly establishes her own private practice. She shares offices with a successful dentist in the Medical Dental Building in downtown Seattle.

Have you ever known a person gifted with the talents of a Jedi Master?

Saving Money for the Grand Circuit

Skippy, Kim, and I meet for drinks at the Red Carpet. I mention a freestyle camp at Palisades Tahoe. Kim thinks she'll go with me next year.

Skippy says he's going to win a trip to Europe selling cars. The prize is actually a trip to Reno with a bunch of Chevy dealers. But that doesn't bother Skippy.

"I can trade it in on a ticket to London," he says. "Why don't you two come with me?"

Humoring Skippy, I say, "Sure, I've never been."

Kim says she's in too.

Skippy's planning the itinerary to include all the places a well-traveled person should see, the grand circuit.

I start saving money.

One's destination is never a place but rather a new way of looking at things.—Henry Miller

What's Wrong with Turning Thirty in Europe?

Skippy calls with good news: he won the contest and is ready to set a date for London. Kim's practice and teaching are taking off, so she opts out. I'm having second thoughts as well due to my trial schedule.

Skippy and I have lunch at Pier 70. We're barely seated when he says, "Ya know, some people talk about doing things, others do them. Which one are you?" A kindhearted judge allows me to try my case in two parts so I can make the trip.

September is a lovely month for European weather, especially in Venice. The American dollar goes far, and we get to stay at the Royal Hotel Danieli, truly a palace.

But spending my thirtieth birthday in Europe should be more wonderful, somehow. I'm out of sorts. It's not my age; I feel like my life is just beginning. Maybe it's because I'm in such romantic places with a platonic companion.

Back in my office, I realize what was wrong on the trip.

New clients come in, worried about a boundary line dispute. I talk with them for ten minutes, check a couple of statutes, and give them my opinion. They leave happy, saying they'll be back if they get any more static from their neighbor.

Here at home, I can count the money, speak the language, find my way without a map. I'm not just another dumb American tourist.

I have found out that there ain't no surer way to find out whether you like people or hate them than to travel with them.—Mark Twain

Our Bodies, Our Rights? Not Quite

As a pioneering female litigator, I'm passionate in my crusade for women's rights. My hero is Gloria Steinem, who is fighting for women's reproductive rights and the right to equal pay.

The 1972 presidential election was brutal for liberals. Women's reproductive issues were excised from the Democratic platform. Our homegrown senator, Henry M. Jackson, came in a distant second to George McGovern as the Democratic nominee. Richard Nixon won by a landslide.

In politics, if you want anything said, ask a man. If you want anything done, ask a woman.—Margaret Thatcher

Ski with Champagne, Sleep in a Bar

Kim is an avid and excellent skier. In Ontario, she skied with members of the Canadian national team on their days off. I'm still a beginner. Nonetheless, she takes me to challenging black runs at Crystal Mountain, buzzing down as I roll my way to the bottom.

We each ski with a backpack. Mine contains a bottle of cheap champagne and a few silver wine goblets. Kim brings cheese and French bread. Sun or snow, we sit on our packs near the top of a run and pop the cork. It draws a crowd, mostly male. I offer a goblet to anyone who seems interesting and looks like he can ski. Twenty minutes later, we're on the hill again with our new friends in tow and a larger audience to watch my embarrassing performance.

Mount Baker, near Bellingham, becomes a favorite haunt. It's one of the snowiest places on Earth. The mountain is the second most active volcano in the Cascades after Mount Saint Helens and second only to Mount Rainier in the size of its glaciers.

Typically, Kim works on Saturday, either at her practice in Seattle or at a practice she establishes in Vancouver, BC. When she works in Seattle, we head out as soon as she's done for the day. We take her 'Vette if we don't have male companions. If guys tag along, I drive the Impala. When it comes to transportation, we like the fact that we're in charge instead of at the mercy of the opposite sex.

Mount Baker has few facilities for overnight stays. Glacier, the nearest approximation of a town, has a grocery store and a well-known bar named Graham's. Convivial owner Gary Graham, a young ex-Boeing engineer, runs this unique establishment with an unusual laid-back gusto. With pool tables and a jukebox, skiers rock the place every Saturday night.

Gary allows a select few patrons, Kim and I among them, to sleep in his rocket ship-like quarters in an attic over the bar where orange shag carpet makes a landing for sleeping bags.

Know your limits. Ski beyond them.

We Can Fix It

At a party on one of our trips to Mount Baker, I see Kim flirting with a big guy, at least 6' 4", with a great physique and sandy blonde hair. He's gorgeous. But he has buck teeth.

I walk over and get Kim's attention out of earshot.

"What are you thinking of doing with that overbite problem?" I whisper.

"We can fix it," she says, rocking her hand in a gesture of equivocation.

I frown, ever skeptical of her dental heroics.

"We can fix it," she repeats.

Later, I realize that "we" includes me.

Kim introduces me to James A. Swan, one of the first freestyle skiers in the Northwest. The next morning, Swan treats us to some of his hottest skiing high jinks, including an airborne somersault over a road. He's soon a member of our pack.

A few weeks later, Kim's "We can fix it" plan is in motion. Swan is lying on my couch, drinking a beer for breakfast. A breakfast beer isn't unusual for him. What's unusual is that he's drinking through a straw.

Kim arranged for his surgery. His jaw is wired shut. She's in charge of continuing care. I'm in charge of convalescence—and straws.

Off the slopes and in recovery, Swan spends his days in front of the TV. We get to know each other well even though he has to talk through clenched teeth.

I learn that his nickname is "Goose." He says his Canadian friends gave it to him.

"My thing was jumping off cliffs, over big trees or into big trees," he says. "Whatever it took to gain recognition in the small audience for early freestyle skiing. Some of my jumps were over a hundred feet high."

Surviving these jumps got him onto the freestyle circuit.

I've heard that Swan was in a few ski films. I ask him if it's true.

"I got my first chance at being in the movies in 1970," he says. "I was living and teaching skiing in Sun Valley. Dick Barrymore and Warren Miller were the major players in ski movies. That's where the story of freestyle skiing started."

Eventually, Swan leaves my couch, heading back to Bellingham and his life of framing houses and freestyle skiing. Of course, he's fallen for Kim along the way, so "we" will stay in touch.

Which sport would you die for?

Grouse Mountain and Whistler

This weekend, Kim practices in Vancouver, BC. A friend of mine who lives in Vancouver takes me skiing at Grouse Mountain.

We ride a tram to the most exquisite Vancouver vista. The lights of the city poke into view—first a few, then dozens, then hundreds and thousands. They feed the flight-like experience of skiing with the joy of looking down at a heaven of simulated stars.

We head back to Vancouver to pick up Kim, get dinner, and hit a few bars. We're headed to Whistler at the crack of dawn, so we hit the sack by 10 p.m. at a friend's apartment, four of us crawling randomly into a huge bed.

It's raining miserably outside. We're an awkward foursome failing to fall asleep. One member of our party, a student from Wyoming, remarks that the rain sounds like a cow pissing on a flat rock. That cracks us up. It's another half hour before we sleep.

Even skiing doesn't change the fact that I'm not a morning person. But Kim is, so we're up and on our way before sunrise. Depending on the weather and how many stops we have to make for road construction and landslides, it's two to three hours to our next skiing adventure.

Skirting the Strait of Georgia, we enjoy a coastal view through the fog of Burrard Inlet and Horseshoe Bay. Then we're on to the picturesque seaside village of Lions Bay on Howe Sound, with its sandy beaches and spectacular views of the Gulf Islands. As we head into dense forests and over creeks, we see "Beware of Bears" signs and cougar cautions.

Then it's on to Squamish, where the ocean meets the Garibaldi Ranges. Once a historic lumber and pulp town, Squamish is now a climbing and hiking mecca. It shares its name with a raging river and the Squamish Nation, descendants of the Coast Salish indigenous peoples.

From here, the road wanders the valley between Cloudburst Mountain on the left and the vast and oppressively rugged Garibaldi Provincial Park on the right. On this overcast early morning, we see lakes of blue, green, and even black.

We arrive at Whistler Village, with its rough-and-ready ticket booths, cafeteria, bar, and other facilities. It was built in just the last ten years on what used to be a garbage dump dominated by black bears. The coastal mountains, with their rugged peaks and hostile landscape, stretch all the way to beautiful Alta Lake just across the highway, but it's obscured in mist today.

My companions zip off to hit Franz's run. I follow the pack, stuttering my way down thirteen hundred vertical feet. In some places, it's groomed; in others, it's bumpy runs with moguls and valleys into which I disappear.

We eat lunch from our packs in the snow. By 3 p.m., the sun breaks through the clouds. Then it's time for a beer at the bottom, followed by the long trudge back to Seattle.

The exhilaration of flying is too keen, the pleasure too great, for it to be neglected as a sport.—Orville Wright

Happy New Year!
(No Diving from the Balcony)

Kim and I throw a New Year's Day brunch at my waterfront apartment. We set up ten cases of champagne on my patio, pouring sacks of ice over the top. As the party gets underway, we move the boxes along the terrace so we can reach out a window to pop another cork. We serve a giant vat of Welsh rarebit with fruit, pastry, and, for Kim, lots of veggies.

Half the guests are lawyers; about a third are dentists. The rest are our ski buddies, plus a small group of eclectic friends we run with. Next year is an election year, so our young mayor, Wes Uhlman, and his wife are here working the crowd.

Wes is one of the best mayors we've ever had. I started working on his campaigns as a teenager. He was running for the legislature while he was still in law school. He was a rising star who quickly got to the top by being on the appropriations committee, where the money is. His DC connections have helped Seattle attract big-dollar projects that wouldn't have been possible without federal funding.

The party lasts through the afternoon until the ten cases of champagne and the food are all gone. By this point, I'm having to get tough to make sure no one, especially my friend Swan, takes a dive into Lake Washington from my third-floor balcony. After all, I'm a personal injury lawyer.

What's the best New Year's Day you can recall?

Ski Racing? Are You Kidding?

Charley brings me an ad for a ski race camp in Palisades Tahoe. I ask him if he's gone crazy. He assures me I don't need to be a racer to run gates. "It's just the best way to get you to make turns when and where you should."

Skeptical but eager to improve my skiing, I fly into Sacramento, rent a car at the Avis "We Try Harder" desk, and head up into the Sierra Nevada mountains. Near the turnoff to I-89, a sign points to Donner Pass, named for George Donner, whose group of Missouri pioneers was stranded in the snow during the brutal winter of 1846-47. They may have resorted to cannibalism to survive. I don't like to think about it.

On I-89, a hundred miles from Sacramento and six thousand feet above sea level, I'm at Palisades Tahoe. This is the biggest area I've ever skied. It was home to the Olympics a dozen or so years ago and, more recently, the World Cup.

I check in and am assigned a roommate, a pleasant woman a little younger than me. At our orientation that night, we meet our coaches. Dick Dorworth runs the camp. He's a world-class skier, coach, and author who once set a world speed record of over a hundred and five miles per hour at Portillo, Chile.

I'm not nearly the oldest ski camper. There's a forty-year-old dentist from Jackson, Mississippi, who's also a race camp newbie. Our coaches are pros, but most of us are beginners, which is a comfort to me.

We learn pre-race focus and how to use mental imagery of the run. A coach tells me, "In the starting gate, pull your upper body out past the start wand before you hit it with your boots. Then pole and skate like crazy until you're moving as fast as you can sprint in track shoes." Other than skiing, I'm completely unathletic; I've never sprinted in track shoes.

I learn that my body will follow my gaze, so I have to be vigilant to keep my eyes on the gate beyond the one I'll turn at next. Or better yet, two gates beyond. "Look up, look up!" I hear many times a day.

It's not cool to quit if we make a mistake. "Grit out the course," one of our coaches says. "No matter how poorly you think you're doing, it's better than a DNF."

Finally, we learn the tuck, otherwise known as the bully or bullet. The purpose is to shave a few tenths of a second off a run. At the bottom of the course, someone yells, "Flatten your skis! Glide and run straight at the last gate." The tuck requires a lot of core strength and lower body strength, along with power and flexibility. Where, I wonder, will I find these attributes before the week is over?

At the end of our last day at camp, some of us feel like celebrating, others feel like commiserating. Both groups head into Tahoe City. Escargots and potato leek soup at the classic Bavarian restaurant follow. A silver moon hangs over the hazy pink sunset on the lake.

When have you felt in over your head but made it anyway?

The Phone Calls

It's September of 1975. Almost my birthday. I get a phone call. It's Harborview Medical Center.

"Dr. Kim Haglund's office gave us your number as an emergency contact. Do you know where she is?"

"I know she's doing a rotation in anesthesia."

"She didn't report in."

Kim has a cardiac arrhythmia disorder. She wears a metal ID bracelet at all times.

I asked Kim about it once and didn't like the answer: "My doctors say I could live to be seventy or die the next minute. There's no way to know and nothing to be done about it."

Maybe that's why Kim lives like there's no tomorrow.

I drive to her Madison Park cottage and pound on the door. No answer. I let myself into the patio and peer through a window.

The bathroom door is partly open. I see her on the floor. My stomach lurches.

She hasn't given me a door key yet or told me where to find one. I look around in panicked futility.

I run next door and ask a woman to call Medic One. While she calls, I ask her young son to come back to Kim's and see if he can get into a tiny back window. I boost him up, he gets the window open, squeezes inside, and comes to the front door to let me in.

I rush to touch her.

I feel her cold body. I see her bluish skin. Her face is purple, her blonde hair splayed.

"No! No! No!" I scream. I feel my own heart squeeze tight.

Then the lawyer in me kicks in.

I take several deep breaths and look for signs of assault. Two five-pound weights are next to the toilet.

Outside, as the firefighters arrive, I shoo the family next door away from the immediate area. They examine Kim. They tell me the police will be here shortly.

Based on Kim's medical history and the condition of her body, the police determine that foul play is unlikely.

I find her address book and start the calls to her family.

Life can change in the blink of an eye,
but love is eternal.—Unknown

Flashbacks

It's been six weeks since Kim's death. I'm still having flashbacks of her on the bathroom floor. The sensations are so strong that if I'm driving, I have to pull over.

I meet with a psychiatrist and tell him that no matter how hard I try to shut them off, the flashbacks keep coming. "Flashbacks are the mind's way to get us to relive the experience," he explains. "Sometimes, we need to re-experience an event until we can accept that it happened. Don't resist. When the flashback comes, stop what you're doing and experience it as though it's coming into the top of your head, flowing through your body, and leaving through your toes." His ideas help me absorb the reality of the loss.

I've never lost anyone so close to me. Never.

I struggle to get back to being productive at work. I resent the happy kids splashing and shouting at the bathing beach next door. My mom encourages me to get a TV and a kitten.

I have a TV but television has never interested me. Now, I watch *All in the Family*, *M*A*S*H*, and *Hawaii Five-O*—anything to avoid thinking. I lie awake at night, listening to the waves hitting the dock until I'm lulled to sleep.

I don't think a kitten is going to help very much.

The inability to get something out of your head is a signal that shouts, "Don't forget to deal with this."—Christina Enevoldsen

10
CHAPTER TEN

Discoveries

One Word

Three months after Kim's death. I'm meeting with my business consultant, Ed Pepin, on a case. It occurs to me to ask him, "Ed, would you consider helping me make my practice more profitable?" He says, "Of course, that's my business."

He asks me about my cases and how I get my referrals.

"Most of my referrals come from former clients and other lawyers," I say. "They tell me that the referring lawyer told them they have a pretty hopeless case, but if anyone could win it, it would be me."

Ed gives me a homework assignment: "In one word, describe how you think your clients and other lawyers see you. Then describe how you see yourself in one word."

Can you describe yourself in one word?
What about others? How do they see you?

From Warrior to Expert

A week later, Ed and I are at 13 Coins. I order black coffee. Ed has his usual hot water and lemon slices. I have my two words.

"Clients see me as their warrior," I tell Ed. "They think I can do the impossible on a shoestring budget. I see myself as an advocate, fearless and skilled in the courtroom."

Ed says, "How do you want to be seen five years from now?"

My answer takes no time: I want to be seen as an expert. I also want a different mix of clients in my personal injury practice. "Having a few impossible cases is fine," I say. "But when they're all impossible, I wake up at 4:30 a.m. like I have weights on my chest."

I realize that I want to be recognized for my expertise and paid for it. In my personal injury practice, I want a few winnable cases in the mix, not just impossible ones.

Together, Ed and I identify a unique skill set I have that's going largely unrecognized.

I got my lowest grade in law school in taxation. But because of some of my early business clients, I have a lot of experience working with the IRS. Along the way, I've learned that taxation is not really about the numbers, which upset me so much. Taxation is about knowing the IRS code, which is nothing but words. Complicated, convoluted words, but still, just words.

What's your expertise?

Another Degree? You're Kidding, Right?

After meeting with Ed for several sessions, we conclude that I should pursue a graduate degree in taxation.

I remember being told in eighth grade that I was "not college material" because my math and science scores were low. Well, I managed to fool them in undergraduate school and even squeak through law school. But am I really going to do this again?

I take control of my thinking. What are the strongest negative thoughts I have about this? What thoughts are so strong they might keep me from getting a master's degree in taxation?

- I'm not smart enough.
- The classes are costly.
- The intense studying will take away from my billable time, reducing my income.
- I'll be miserable having to study again.
- I'm not good at concentrating.
- It'll take years. I'll be over forty before I get this degree.
- It'll ruin my social life.

I decide I can handle the costs by taking night classes even though it will take a lot longer. I figure I'll be forty at some point anyway. Might as well be forty with a tax degree.

Wrinkles will only go where the smiles have been.—Jimmy Buffett

The Power of Positive Thinking

I need to acknowledge my negative thoughts. But I also need to support my positive thinking, so I create the following affirmations:

- I'm a fully qualified tax expert.
- I'm an eager student with excellent study habits.
- Taxation comes easily to me.
- I concentrate instantly on the subject at hand.
- I always go straight to the heart of the matter.
- My recall is excellent; I have a great head for figures.
- I easily harmonize my tax studies with work and my social life.
- Graduate school adds spice, zest, and excitement to my life.
- I'm a gifted, talented, and happy straight-A student.

I also set a few rules for myself.

- I do all my schoolwork in my time away from the office.
- I allow myself one day of work time per semester to study for an exam or finish a paper.
- I'll gain time by resigning from several nonprofit boards and giving up certain political activities.

My first classes are enjoyable. I'm in the company of accountants and a few other lawyers. Our professors are top-notch tax attorneys. They work in the real world of tax law on problems I already deal with or will soon encounter.

I look for a book to improve my studying. I find good advice from a kindred positive thinker in Melvin Powers' book *A Guide to Better Concentration*.

While reading it, I discover that I already have many of the concentration skills he recommends. In addition to providing practical suggestions, he promotes affirmations, which he calls self-suggestion, visualization, and self-inspiration.

I inspire myself by thinking of Marie Curie, the extraordinary scientist. I'm also inspired by environmentalist Rachel Carson, author of *Silent Spring.* What concentration those two women must have cultivated.

Sure enough, my attitude is now positive, and I look forward to each class.

Have you ever made affirmations and read them faithfully every day?

A Ski Week Fling

Spring 1977. Swan lives in Park City, Utah, now with his girlfriend, Janet, who works full-time and probably pays the rent. Fred, one of our skiing pack, has spring break from college. If I take my Porsche, he'll do some of the driving.

There's a collection of male skiers at Janet's apartment to drink and visit with us new arrivals. These guys are all too young for me but oh so attractive.

Swan introduces me to a guy named Chuck. He's tall and handsome, but he doesn't seem to talk. And there's the age difference, of course. Still, for a ski week fling...

Today, Chuck drops by to give us a lift to the hill in his Jeep. As I start to heft my skis to the roof, this guy who doesn't talk whisks them from my hands and carefully places them in the rack.

I time the chairlift for a chance to ride up with Chuck. He actually speaks! I turn and notice his blue eyes: like snow reflecting the sky and dark lashes to envy.

He explains that he's taking a semester off from the University of Arizona. His father works in Park City, managing the mine under the ski slope. Chuck has free room and board. Last summer, he worked at the mine as a laborer, which might explain his lean, muscular physique.

Love comes when you least expect it.
Love comes when you most need it.—Mitch Albom

When the Rest of the Room Disappears

I can't get enough of this shy ski bum. He was a little timid with me at first because he thought I was Fred's date. Since that got straightened out, we've been inseparable.

Sitting in the bar after skiing today, I could have sworn the rest of the room—all the people and even the music—disappeared. There was only Chuck.

Tomorrow, Fred and I head back to Seattle. I wish I could stay longer, but I have a trial.

Chuck invites me over to his dad's elegant home. His dad is out of town and I can even get a hot shower. No such luck in the shower traffic jam at Swan's.

After the shower, we relax in the conversation pit, listening to Joan Armatrading's "Water with the Wine." Seduction follows.

Now I'm looking into his eyes, and he asks me, "Why so sad?"

I whisper, "Because I'll never see you again."

"Why do you say that?" he asks.

"I'm sure that when the next ski bus arrives, there'll be another ski bunny here."

"What bus?" he asks.

He promises to visit me in Seattle.

Shall I stay? Would it be a sin? If I can't help falling in love with you?
—Elvis Presley

The Odd Couple

Chuck is visiting me in Seattle as promised. But, already, complications have arisen.

Mom and Dad had a fire at their condo. They're sleeping in my bedroom while I sleep on the couch until repairs are made. I've arranged for Chuck to stay downstairs with my friend Rick, a physician who works the ER forty-eight on and forty-eight off.

We get some time alone at Rick's, but it seems odd. It's the age difference. Chuck is eight years younger than I am. This didn't seem strange in Park City, but now Mom wants to know who this "boy" is.

At my office, his jeans, cowboy boots, and Pendleton shirt seem odd in relation to my Ralph Lauren jacket, pencil skirt, and stilettos.

I agree to visit him in Tucson, where he's going back to college. He's studying to be a programmer, whatever that is.

Programmer: A machine that turns coffee into code.—Unknown

A Strange Journey of Self-Discovery

Summer 1977. I'm in a room with a couple hundred people. We sit in folding chairs with our eyes closed. Our male facilitator, Randy, begins our next activity. I'm sure he's on his high stool up front, a maroon Bally shoe perched on the rung, Dior stitched over blue dress socks.

He's worn something different each day. He looks like a Wall Street bond trader recently returned from a Bermuda vacation.

His sandy hair is short and blown dry with volume, as promised by the shampoo ads. The program brochure notes his PhD. I suspect it's a PhD in marketing—not psychology, as he would have us believe.

Cara, his female counterpart, says, "Breathe deeply, centering your mind where you feel tension, discomfort, or pain." I hear the tinkle of the gold charm bracelet she wears as she quietly prowls the back of the room, her kelly-green pumps tossed into a corner.

We exhale audibly and settle into our bodily sensations. I know Cara's credentials. She's a PhD candidate.

I place my hand awkwardly at the back of my neck between my shoulder blades. *How did I get myself into this four-day marathon?* My sweater feels nubby. I'm warm and prickly in this body among bodies. Something brushes my leg. My neighbor's skirt?

Randy speaks: "Remove your hand now and bring the discomfort, pain, tension, or whatever you feel into your lap. With your eyes still closed, examine what is in your hand. What is its shape? Is it hard or soft?"

It was Ed Pepin, my business consultant, who got me into this. He's done the program. He assured me it would do wonders for my practice and help me find just the right relationship. "Don't ask questions," he said. "Just fork over the $600 and do it."

I hear Cara's bracelet jingle up by the stool. Obediently, I search my palm with my mind's eye. The tension between my shoulders feels hard, angular, jagged.

Cara notices my discomfort. In a whisper, she asks, "Does it have a color?"

Battleship gray.

"Is it big or small?"

Dagger size.

A cello intrudes through four giant speakers, creating a concert-like feeling.

Randy continues, "Take the object in your palm and hold it out chest-high. In your other hand, notice that you have a glass beaker. If your object is solid, imagine it as a liquid and pour it into the beaker. If it is a liquid, imagine it is in the beaker and pour it out into a solid. Now look at it again."

His words rush up with a crescendo of violins.

"What color, shape, size, or consistency do you see?"

How good is your imagination?

In the Middle

The music stops. Cara speaks softly: "Think back now to your earliest childhood experiences and register the first thing that comes into your mind."

I'm five years old. I'm in the living room of our old apartment at Burien Gardens. It's long and narrow and has a braided rug of many colors, the kind pioneers made from old rags.

Dad's at the other end of the room, holding in one hand his black metal lunch pail shaped like a mailbox. He's thin with wavy black hair and a handsome face, except maybe for his beaky nose.

He's wearing a work shirt and slacks. Mom is wearing a cotton house dress with an apron and a headscarf. She's been cleaning since she got home from working at the drugstore.

Dad's bracing as Mom starts to yell. I don't know what he's done this time, but it sounds bad. Mom's smoking a cigarette; the smoke is going into her eyes. She looks like she's breathing fire.

I pull my rocking chair out of the middle of the room, set my Teddy bear, TB, in it, and put my sweater over his head.

I run over to Dad and put my arm around his leg. I can feel the top of his work boot where the laces stop.

Mom is standing by her "whatnot cupboard." Teensy cups she calls demitasses and the mustache cup from her grandfather live there. Also a cranberry glass decanter and stemmed wine glasses from her great-aunt Berry.

Mom seems so far away now and so mad. I'm afraid she'll explode. Dad says, "Aw, Janice. C'mon now, honey. Calm down."

This just makes Mom madder. Her face is turning red like the lipstick she's wearing that I always see on the cigarette butts in the ashtrays.

I run sideways between the rug and the wall. She just waxed the floors, and my black patent shoes are slippery.

I get to Mom and grab her apron, trying to get her attention. "Don't be mad, Mom," I plead, choking on my tears.

She has a demitasse cup in her hand from the whatnot. I skitter along the path between the rug and wall, past TB again, and pull on Dad's pant leg. "Dad, do something! Don't let Mom be mad."

His face is angry now, but he's still pleading. "Janice, this is nonsense. Don't carry on like this. You're just upsetting yourself."

Back across the chasm I go toward Mom as I hear the first pathetic crash of a tiny antique cup.

"Aw shit, Janice. What'd you have to do that for?"

"What do you care? They're not *your* things. I'm the only one around here who cares about making a home for this family."

I slide into her leg, bracing myself against the white nurse's shoes she wears to work in. I feel her body surge with power as she sweeps the whatnot cupboard from the wall, its precious cargo crashing to the floor, a sickening sound of crystal shattering.

Mom sinks to the ground, sobbing into my ringlets as I put my arms around her shoulders. Dad strides across the long room and starts cleaning up the mess, righting the whatnot and picking out the few cups and glasses that have survived.

"Get Daddy the broom, honey," he says to me, muted and sad. "And bring Mommy a hankie."

*Battling is a way to show, no matter what,
that you both will stick together forever.—Unknown*

A Pattern from My Past

Jim Croce sings from the four speakers, "If I could save time in a bottle…" Cara's voice coos over the melody: "Look at your life today. Do you see anything like what you saw in your early childhood experiences? If not, that's OK. Just be where you are right now."

Croce promises, "I'd spend all my days with you." His voice is sweet. It reminds me of the last time I heard the song at a friend's wedding.

"Are you repeating a pattern you learned in childhood?" Randy asks. "Are you carrying pain in order to hold onto something? Or to make up for something missing? Someone who should have been there but wasn't?

Think about it over this next fifteen-minute break. This will be a silent break. No talking. When we come back, we'll do some sharing."

I hear the scrape of two hundred chairs as I rise with the others. I wish I had my watch, but they made us turn them in at the door. I remember I promised Mom that I'd come over to their place tonight and try to talk some sense into Dad. She's upset with him because he insists on keeping this job in Steilacoom, and it's a two-and-a-half-hour commute every day. She says I'm the only one who can get through to him.

I wish she'd leave me out of it.

Now I understand my childhood memories. I've always put myself in the middle of disputes, trying to resolve them. No wonder I'm an attorney.

What do you let others put you in the middle of?

11
CHAPTER ELEVEN

Taking a Chance on Love

A Frivolous Relationship

I think a lot about Chuck, but it's a frivolous relationship. I'm a thirty-four-year-old career woman. He's twenty-six and still taking college courses.

I plan my trip to Tucson for Labor Day weekend so I don't miss work and Chuck doesn't have classes.

Chuck studies computer science, but the University of Arizona doesn't offer a computer science undergraduate program. So he has to take some of this and some of that to get the skills he needs.

It's my first trip to Tucson. The heat shimmers off the blacktop as Chuck drives from the airport to his parents' house.

Chuck's mom, dad, and brother live in Park City. He and his sister Margie live in Tucson. The house is a smart ranch-style with bedrooms for a family of six and a backyard that's mostly patio and swimming pool.

Chuck's sister and a friend, Joel, go for a run in the relative cool of the morning. By my standards, it's still blazing hot, so I change into a bathing suit and slather on sunblock.

I bounce around in the water while Chuck swims laps. I took years of grade-school swim lessons in the summer rain at Angle Lake near Sea-Tac Airport, but my skills never matured much beyond face float, back float, and dog paddle.

We'll visit the Desert Museum tomorrow, so we grab dinner and turn in early—at least that's the excuse.

Have you ever continued a relationship,
feeling an unyielding force against all odds?

Chocolate-Covered Bananas and Impossible Romance

Chuck tells me that the Desert Museum covers nearly a hundred acres of regional plants, animals, and geological specimens curated from the Sonoran Desert. We'll see only a tiny part today.

The museum's founders wanted to overcome the lack of knowledge about the desert locally and nationally. It's unlike any museum or zoo I've ever visited. I'm the perfect blank slate.

The exquisite art of the Tohono O'odham basket weavers fascinates me. Stunning gems and fossils illuminate dim memories of an undergraduate geology course. The arthropods, from spiders to scorpions, creep me out. It's a day of endless discovery and childlike fascination.

When we can't walk anymore, we head for the car, which is blazing hot. On the way home, we stop for ice cream. I'm delighted by the chocolate-covered frozen banana, which combines my two favorite foods. We don't have these in Seattle.

Our time together passes too quickly. Before I know it, I'm on the plane home, thinking about chocolate-covered bananas and Chuck, my latest impossible romance.

Who let the cougar out of the bag?

Strong Language, High Stakes

I agree to participate as a pro bono lawyer in a first-degree aggravated murder case. John R. is the lead attorney. This is a capital case, a botched bank robbery where a deputy sheriff was killed. Seven defendants face the death penalty.

I've never worked on a capital case before and wouldn't attempt to do so without John R. in the lead. I represent the three least culpable defendants. I know the days will be long and stressful, but I hunger for the experience.

Organizing a conference with all seven defendants requires special arrangements. The judge facilitates this so John R. and I can advise all of our clients at the same time about how they should behave in the courtroom. John R. speaks to this as directly as possible.

"I don't know what you were doing, robbing a bank with seven people and only a vague idea of an escape route. But I'm here to save your lives.

"If you've noticed how police officers look at you, you know how strongly they feel about the loss of their fellow officer and friend. Jurors will be aware of this too. So you will do exactly what I'm about to tell you every time we enter the courtroom.

"You will be unshackled and seated before the jury is allowed to enter. When the jurors come in, you will stand and look generally in their direction without making eye contact with any individual member.

"When the jury is seated, turn your chair straight forward, face the judge, and don't look at the jury again. Look at the judge, look at me, or look at the prosecutor. Don't pick at your fingernails or crack your knuckles. Don't laugh at any jokes or make any faces.

"If a bank teller points to you and says that you're the guy who was wearing purple shoes, don't jump up and shout that they were green. If you don't want to be hanged before the verdict, whatever anyone says, don't speak."

The roughest roads often lead to the top.—Christina Aguilera

That Strange Feeling

Just before Christmas 1978. I've been dating again. This time, it's a dentist named Vern. I haven't talked to Chuck in over a year, but I haven't stopped thinking about him either. I have a propensity for impossible relationships. I think I've used this to avoid commitment.

I call Chuck's house in Park City a little late at night, hoping I don't wake his parents. He answers on the second ring. He says he knew it was me. We talk for a long time.

I tell him I'm going to Sun Valley for Christmas via charter with my mentor, John R., and his crew. Chuck says there's no snow in Sun Valley; we should come to Park City, where conditions are great.

The next day, on our way to Sun Valley, I mention to John R. that a friend in Utah says there's no snow there. As we fly in, we see that the mountains are bare. John R. asks the captain to take us to Utah.

I call Chuck and ask him if he can find accommodations for the five of us on the flight. I wait by the pay phone. Ten minutes later, he calls back.

"I can get you into the three-bedroom condo my dad and I lived in before, but only until Christmas Day," he says. "Then you'll have to move."

John R. says, "We'll take it."

I'd planned to meet Vern, the dentist I'm dating, in Sun Valley after Christmas. I call to tell him of the change of plans. "No problem," he says. "I'll meet you in Park City instead."

Chuck joins the five of us for dinner, along with Swan and Janet. John R., being his usual magnanimous self, orders food and drink for the whole crowd on his tab.

Chuck is no longer a ski bum. He has a haircut and a job as a software engineer in Salt Lake City. John R. makes a few polite inquiries of Chuck but doesn't give him the third degree. He then turns his attention to his latest girlfriend, Luanne, a flight attendant.

I mention to Chuck that a friend of mine, Vern, is coming in the day after Christmas. I'm hoping Chuck gets the message that I'm available only for a limited time.

Suddenly, I have that strange feeling that everything except Chuck is disappearing again. When the party breaks up, he says he'll drive me home, but we decide on a detour to a nice motel away from downtown. The time we've been apart evaporates. We melt into each other completely.

On Christmas Day, we ski and have dinner at Chuck's, where I meet his family for the first time. His parents and brother live in a farm-style house on a large lot being encroached upon by upscale condos and apartments in the building boom.

Chuck's mother is a warm homemaker, obviously proud of her brood. His dad is all business, orchestrating activities. His twin sisters are whip-smart. One is becoming a chemical engineer, the other an agronomist. His brother, ten years younger, is still in high school.

Finally, there's the traditional Christmas family photo, which includes strays, like me, who have wandered in.

Family is not an important thing. It's everything.—Michael J. Fox

God, If You'll Get Me Out of This...

Swan offers to cook dinner the next night for everyone at the condo we're now renting. He invites Chuck to join us. Uh-oh. Vern will be here before dinner. What am I going to do now?

I mention to Chuck that my friend is coming but that I think he'll beg off on dinner. It doesn't happen. Vern shows up announcing that his divorce became final that day, so he's celebrating. He proceeds to get plastered. Sarcastic remarks from John R. go over Vern's head.

As the dinner guests leave, I walk Chuck to the door. I look into his eyes and make a silent deal with God: "God, get me out of this, and I'll never do it again." As we mumble our goodnights, Chuck looks hurt, which wounds me too.

Vern is hungover in the morning but game to ski. I call Chuck's house to see if he's coming. His mom says he's gone to meet his friend Dave. When Vern and I show up, Chuck and Dave are sprawled at a table in the ticket plaza in front of the coffee shop. I'm surprised they didn't head up without us.

I introduce Vern to Dave, our breath visible on this below-zero day. Chuck says nothing to me. We head up the mountain and, after a few runs, Vern gets out his flask and offers it around. Chuck declines, but I accept, hoping it will make me less tense in this unbearably awkward situation. I'm with the guy I don't want to be with, watching the guy I want to be with get more pissed off by the minute.

Finally, as we start down, Chuck says to me, "You need to go in and get your ears warm." Slightly buzzed by the rum, I argue that I'm fine, warm even. In his grouchiest voice, Chuck commands, "If you want to have anything left to hang earrings on, you will go in. Now."

We head to the nearest mountain cafeteria. Once inside, my ears start hurting like crazy as they thaw. Vern invites me to join him for the Rose Bowl in Pasadena; he's flying out tonight. I tell him I need to head back to Seattle with John R.'s crew to prepare for a case going to trial on Tuesday.

After skiing, John R. has a chat with me.

"Get rid of the dentist," he says. "Marry this guy, Chuck."

"Why?" I ask, astonished.

"Can't you tell he adores you?"

"No," I say. Especially not today, when I think he hates me.

"You haven't noticed, have you?"

"Noticed what?"

"When you're in a crowded room, he knows where you are at all times."

John R. is the best judge of character I know. He said he'd pick my husband when he thought I was ready for marriage.

"I don't think Chuck's speaking to me right now," I say.

"I'll take care of that," John R. says, heading for a phone.

John R.'s crew has assembled at a trendy restaurant for our bon voyage dinner. Chuck got the message John R. left for him and has appeared right on time. As usual, John R. handles the seating, putting Chuck and me together. Chuck whispers, "I had to show up out of respect for John R."

I know I'm not out of the woods yet, but I feel like God's going to fulfill my bargain.

Have you ever made a deal with God? How did it go?

Reconnecting, Reconsidering

I get a letter from Chuck. We make plans for me to visit his family for Presidents' Day weekend, but he wants to see me sooner. He's working for a company in Salt Lake City that does business with a company in New Hampshire, where he needs to head for a week.

Reworking his itinerary, Chuck routes himself through Seattle on his way back. He stays the weekend.

My perspective on Chuck is changing. Given our age difference and the fact that Chuck is all science and I'm all words, I've always assumed our relationship was for the moment, not long term. Now that he has a haircut, a job, and John R.'s blessing, I think I may need to reconsider my assumption.

A drop of pure love contains an ocean of transformative power.
—Adiela Akoo

The Charm, the Lake, the Plumbing

I've been preoccupied with buying a cottage on Lake Washington. It's a charming little house with leaded glass windows, a great view of the lake, and a dock in good condition.

Before the purchase, Mom, the realtor, makes her inspection. Dad, the plumber, offers his expertise. "There's running water in the basement," he says. "Not through the pipes, but we can fix that."

I dive in, confident that any house on the lake under a hundred thousand dollars is a good investment.

What's the best investment you've ever made?

Empty Fridge, Full Hearts

Unlike Chuck's last Seattle trip, when my parents occupied my apartment due to a fire at their condo, we have absolute privacy at my little cottage by the lake. It's not elegantly decorated like my Madison Park apartment was, but it's charming and cozy.

On Saturday, we go to Lake City for donuts and coffee. Then we return home to spend the afternoon lounging, admiring the water and each other. By late afternoon, we're hungry again.

Chuck looks in the refrigerator and laughs. "Don't you ever eat?" he asks. "You have one bottle of green olives with only one olive in it."

He opens a cupboard and finds plenty of food for my Siamese cat. Another cupboard has four boxes of Cheerios, the mainstay of the rare dinners I eat at home when I've remembered to stop for milk.

Neither of us is in the mood for Cheerios and a green olive, so we head to Madison Park, my old neighborhood, to dine at The Attic, an exceptional burger place that serves prime rib on Saturday night.

On Sunday, we sleep in. I need to catch up from the hours I've been putting into my capital case. Later, we do a little sightseeing and return in the afternoon before Chuck's 7:00 p.m. flight. Waylaid by lust, we rush to the airport but arrive a few minutes too late.

I hear my name being paged and pick up a white courtesy phone. My answering service connects me to Swan.

"Where are you?" he asks. "Vern, Fred, and I are at the Red Carpet. Come have dinner with us."

Swan prides himself on being able to con my answering service to connect him for an emergency every time.

"I'm at the airport. Chuck just missed his flight,"

"Great. Bring him along."

I tell Swan that I'll check with Chuck and that if we're coming, we'll be there in twenty minutes. I ask Chuck if he has any interest in dinner with Swan, Vern, and Fred. Chuck smiles and, to my surprise, says, "Sure."

By the time we arrive at the Red Carpet, we're way behind in the beer drinking. Chuck sits close to me, across from Vern. He seems to enjoy being the one with the girl this time. Per John R.'s orders and my all-consuming infatuation with Chuck, I haven't dated Vern since I returned from Park City.

Chuck negotiates with his company to stay a few days extra and accompanies me to trial in Tacoma. Surprised but delighted, John R. greets him enthusiastically.

We're selecting jurors, not the most exciting part of a trial. Still, Chuck gets to see some strategy and psychology at work. After two intense days, I take Chuck to the airport.

A few days later, I receive a heartfelt letter. Chuck talks of our worlds, how different they are and yet somehow complementary. To my surprise and delight, he opens up more in print than in person about his feelings.

Ever missed a plane and been glad you did?

The Verdict

I wish Chuck could have been here for the part of the trial when John R. offered expert witness testimony on the shooting. Based on the ballistics, John R. argues that it's more likely than not that the bullet that killed the deputy sheriff was crossfire from the gun of a state patrol officer who came late to the scene.

We wait for the verdict. John R. thinks all seven of the defendants have a chance of avoiding the death penalty. Four were caught in the act. The other three took part in the planning. There's no way any of them will avoid the robbery charge.

If the jury finds that any defendant committed first-degree aggravated murder, all defendants can be found guilty. If the jury finds the defendants guilty of felony murder, the death penalty does not apply. If the jury feels that reasonable doubt exists about who fired the shot that killed the deputy sheriff, they should acquit all defendants on the aggravated murder charges.

After two days of deliberation, we're called back to receive the verdict. The jury hands the verdict to the judge. He reviews it and hands it to the bailiff, who reads, "As to the count of first-degree aggravated murder, we, the jury, find the defendants not guilty. As to the count of felony murder, we, the jury, find the defendants guilty."

Tonight, we help the defendants understand the verdict and the likely sentences they will face. The death penalty is off the table. The two defendants most likely to have been found guilty of aggravated murder are palpably relieved.

We explain that each of the defendants will likely serve twenty years in prison for the felony murder with eight years off for good behavior. The robbery counts will be served concurrently. My three clients stand a chance of receiving a lesser sentence.

John R. and I are too tired to celebrate, so he heads for his hotel, and I head home to Seattle. I call Chuck and give him the good news.

Nothing is more excruciating than waiting for the jury's verdict. Except, perhaps, hearing the jury's verdict.—Richard Paul Evans

Guess Who's Coming to Dinner?

Presidents' Day weekend comes quickly, and here I am back in Park City. I have my own room at the farmhouse, across the hall from Chuck's. There's a good bit of sneaking back and forth—while trying to be discreet, of course.

The problem is Tennille, the Great Dane, who watches Chuck's every move. If we were in my room with the door closed, Tennille's whining and scratching at the door would give us away. So I sneak into Chuck's room. He gets Tennille to lie on her bed in the corner.

In the evening, I realize I'm surrounded by incredibly intelligent people as dinner table discussion bounces briskly from topic to topic. First it's the environment. Then it's sustainable agriculture in West Africa. Next up? Basketball scores.

It doesn't seem to matter what we talk about, everyone has something to say. Intimidated by Chuck's dad, who has strong opinions to share about everything, I hold my tongue, trying my best to fit in.

I enjoy time in the kitchen with Chuck's mother. She's an avid letter writer to friends and relatives and has beautiful handwriting. I think of all the friends I don't keep in contact with. Maybe part of it is my lousy left-handed handwriting. More likely, it's laziness.

The bond that links your true family is not one of blood, but of respect and joy in each other's life.—Richard Bach

A Worthy Gamble

Back in Seattle, getting letters from Chuck is the best part of my week. His letters are romantic and intimate now.

I get one today, written right after I left Park City. It's the first one I've received signed, "Love, Chuck."

I've invited Chuck to come live with me just for the summer. I've never lived with anyone; neither has he.

He accepts.

This is scary, but I think it's a worthy gamble on a sweet romance.

When have you gambled on romance?

12
CHAPTER TWELVE

An Ending and a Beginning

A Helluva Time Heli-Skiing

February 1979. Months ago, before reconnecting with Chuck in Park City, I promised to go with Vern on a helicopter ski trip in March. Now I'm seeing Chuck, and Vern is seeing a woman he met with Swan at Crystal Mountain.

Vern and I made our nonrefundable deposits last fall, so we decide to go as platonic friends. I talk it over with Chuck. He's OK with it.

I wake to the whir and whap of rotors in the frosty fog. I wonder how Vern can sleep through a helicopter passing over close enough to shake this dilapidated old hotel.

Ten minutes later, the helicopter circles again. This means that higher up on the mountain, where we'll be skiing, the fog has lifted.

I hop out of bed, my feet hitting the freezing linoleum floor. I reach for the single lamp in the room and look around on the floor for my goose-down slippers.

I ruffle Vern's hair, trying to rouse him. The helicopter is making its third pass. We're a go.

I dive into my carefully stacked layers and silk long johns. I threaten Vern with bodily harm if he doesn't get up by the time I get back from the loo.

The best Vern can do this morning is offer a "Hrumpffff." I grab my makeup kit and head into the icy hall.

"Vern," I plead. "The helicopter made its third circle fifteen minutes ago. If you want breakfast before the bus leaves, you'll have to move it."

"Third circle," he slurs.

He rolls over the edge of the bed, bringing most of the bedding with him.

"Holy mother, that's cold," he says.

"They're acclimating us for the day," I reply.

"I hear that the temperature with wind chill is minus forty."

Hank yells into our room, "C'mon you luv birds, stop gettin' it on and get out here if you want to catch some vertical. Bus leaves in thirty minutes."

"I gotta piss like Snoqualmie Falls," says Vern, pulling on his stretch bibs.

"You'll have to wait in line," shouts Hank.

I grab my fanny pack and stuff in my gloves, goggles, neck gaiter, and runaway straps. The last and most important item, my Pieps, I sling around my neck and tuck into my jacket. The lifesaving transceiver feels cold and hard against my chest. But not as cold and hard as life would be if I were underneath an avalanche and no one could find me.

I sit next to Nels, our guide, carefully digging out my soft-boiled egg from the shell without oozing yolk on the white linen tablecloth.

"Picked any runs?" I ask him.

"Not yet. Need samples," he says. "The copter's on a checkout now. Probably the Monashees. Wind's blowing from the Caribou side. Looks good for visibility above fifteen hundred feet. Gunther and Wilhelm are on the glacier taking samples."

Smelling of lime shaving cream, Vern shows up for the breakfast I've assembled for him. He pitched this trip when we were out on my dock in ninety-degree weather last summer. He explained that the Rocky Mountain Surgical Dental Society is an organization dedicated to skiing in exotic places and writing it off for tax purposes. He said they'd put up with one lawyer if I plunked down my $1500.

"Better be prepared to take the heat for the entire malpractice crisis," Vern threatens lightheartedly.

I offer a seminar on avoiding malpractice as fluff to cover the boondoggle.

What has been your best boondoggle ever?

Atop the Roof of Canada, I Stand Triumphant

"Everybody got Pieps?" Nels yells from the front. "Check your neighbor."

Midway back in the bus, there's a groan. An orthopedist careens down the middle aisle to hoots and hollers. Five minutes later, we bounce down the rutted two-lane road to the airstrip. In Blue River in March, there's nothing left of winter snow but dirty piles of small brown sand dunes.

We gather on the tarmac, watching the orange windsock standing at attention in the steady gusts. A few small planes covered with tarps are the only evidence of aviation.

Anticipation is high for our first taste of snow. It's fifteen minutes to sunrise when the chopper sets down to pick up passengers. The disappointment of yesterday's grounding due to fog is forgotten.

Nels looks like a conquering warrior. He has a sixty-pound pack slung carelessly over one shoulder, his face peeking out from the oval of the hood in his mountaineering parka. His breath forms ice crystals as he herds us together for his briefing.

He hefts a stack of two dozen black ski poles and offers them around. I wonder for a moment, in this mostly tall group of men, what I, at 5' 3", will do with a six-foot ski pole. Then Nels leans over, twists the grip, and telescopes it at a ninety-degree angle to my arm. "Perfect, thanks," I whisper.

All of a sudden, Nels yells over the din of excited skiers, "Pieps check, people!" He doesn't have our full attention. "Listen up, your life may depend on it. More importantly, since I go first, mine might."

One at a time, each skier walks to the other side of the runway with Pieps on send while we all listen on receive. Nels drills us for ten minutes on what an avalanche grid search looks like. I now understand the need for poles that extend to six feet. Next, it's shoveling procedures.

Sobered by the reality of the risks, we all stand quieter as the copter comes in for the pickup. Helicopter drills consume another ten minutes. The guide and the pilot take turns explaining details like how to avoid getting beheaded by a rotor.

"Avoid wrecking the chopper by holding your skis upright with the rotor turning," says the pilot. "And don't get fried by walking into the temperature probe."

We practice turtle walking for pickup and rolling away after landing. The sun is up now, blazing over the frost and fog in fingers through low clouds.

I'm seated in the copter, looking backward. I watch Blue River run away from us as we skim over the long-needled pines toward the Monashee Mountains.

I mull over the wisdom of making this trip. I was a little unnerved to find that there was only one other woman here and she didn't come to ski. Vern has assured me I'm up to this. This company has had a couple of scary rescues but never a fatality.

We burst through a thick layer on takeoff. When I look back, I see nothing but a sea of cottage cheese falling away as we climb.

It's a short ride, and then we're out of the helicopter. I see nothing but the tops of mountains in every direction. I hear nothing but the squeak of ski boots as skiers quietly mount skis and fix runaway straps.

"No one starts down until I give the word," Nels says. "Go left, and we'll pick you up next summer."

We're perched on a ledge about fifty feet wide, with orange streamers marking the landing site.

"Everyone, right behind me," Nels orders, shouldering the heavy pack. "Kurt, pick up the red pack and come last," he says to an Austrian mountain-climbing guide from Innsbruck who's here for a week.

I deliberately refrain from looking over the edge to see where we're going. I concentrate on Vern's skis in front of me, anticipating the next turn from the rhythm he sets with his wild, slightly out-of-control style. We're in a narrow chute with rocky outcroppings on both sides, "sphincter country," as they call it. *Some first run*, I think, glad that I have my new quick-turning skis.

The chute is short and steep. For a few moments I can't tell what's beyond it, until I see an hourglass rock formation ahead where everyone has stopped in a bunch. I'm second to last in front of Kurt. If I fall, he'll be my only witness. My skis hold while I make a few stabbing turns, panic replacing form. The snow is wind-packed and crusty, not what we came for.

At the opening of the hourglass, we stop, mesmerized. There before us is a beautiful, gently rolling glacier spread like French vanilla ice cream as far as the eye can see.

"This has already been scouted, but I'll go first," says Nels. "When I stop and cross my poles, you can come after, making tracks no further than six feet on either side of mine. That's for two reasons. First, I know where the crevasses are, and you don't. They range from small ones of thirty feet to several hundred feet deep. I carry ninety feet of rope in the pack. Second, there's a group coming immediately after us, so let's not pig the powder."

I twist my goggles around to the back of my neck, dig out the Vuarnet shades from my fanny pack, and dab some SPF 25 sunscreen on my nose. Nels cuts perfect figure eights in the fresh powder, stopping five hundred feet below us and giving a clear signal. In pairs, we follow, laying down parallel squiggles.

I take three turns and plop into the new snow, unaccustomed to the unrestrained sensation of fresh powder. The terrain isn't difficult, and I quickly get my rhythm, more comfortable now that I've already goofed.

As we ski up to Nels, he points thirty feet to our left. There's a gaping crevasse, invisible to the untrained eye. If it wasn't clear a few minutes ago, it certainly is now: these guides earn their money.

A giddy lightheartedness overtakes me, replacing the in-over-my-head emotions I had during avalanche training this morning. Atop the roof of Canada, I stand triumphant!

Heli-skiing is all about living through a white blaze of speed and thrill.
—*Unknown*

A New Goal

I'm taking an efficiency class someone recommended called "More Time, Good Time." Because much of my work is by the hour, I need to use my time as effectively as possible. But the class seems to be more about goal setting than time management.

I already have written goals, so I tally what's not written but is on my mind. As a liberated woman, I've pretty much decided marriage is off the table. If I can earn my own living, what's the point? Isn't marriage just a trap to keep women in the kitchen and under the thumb?

Lately, however, my biological clock seems to have kicked in, and I've started to notice babies. I'm even a homeowner now. There's also something more appealing about the idea of building a life with someone. So I'm writing a new goal: someone to love and to love me. I don't use the word "marriage." That's scary. But I catalog the attributes of my ideal mate.

When we started this assignment, no one mentioned that we'd be reading our goals aloud to our classmates. When it's my turn, I read my list of attributes (with a few censored). One I read out is, "An enthusiastic skier and someone who likes to travel and play seriously." From the back of the room, I hear a deep masculine voice ask, "Downhill or cross-country?" The room laughs, but the point is well taken. Goals need to be specific. I quickly answer, "Downhill."

Do you have written goals? Do you read them every day?

It Was the "Normal" One in the Family

March 18, 1979. Out of nowhere comes a fatal heart attack. My brother Tim is dead.

Pat is at the hospital with Tim's wife, Jadanne. He wants me to get Mom and Dad, who are taking beginning ski lessons at Snoqualmie Pass.

I'm shocked beyond belief. I just saw Tim, Jadanne, and the kids, Steve and Sabrina, last night. Tim told me about the Tacoma St. Patrick's Day half-marathon he'd just run. They came to bring me my belated Christmas present, a stepladder I'd asked for now that I'm a homeowner.

I scramble for clothes, then ski boots, purse, car keys, and my wits. As I drive the hour to Snoqualmie, I try to wrap my mind around what has happened and rehearse the ways I can tell my sixty-year-old parents that their thirty-eight-year-old son is dead.

Tim was the one with the Type B personality. He never smoked, and he drank only moderately. He was a machinist with a wife, two kids, and a paid-for house.

Pat is the Type A personality, the high-powered Boeing contract administrator with a herd of lawyers working for him. He travels the world, meeting with foreign leaders.

Had the news been about Pat, my heart would have been just as broken, but I wouldn't have been so thoroughly surprised. Had it been me, heli-skiing last week.... But it wasn't. It was the "normal" one in the family. It was Tim.

Mom and Dad see me walk up to them as they come down from their lesson. Immediately, they know something bad has happened.

I gather up their things and take them to my car.

I begin my well-rehearsed story.

Tim woke up, said to his wife that his arms felt heavy, then collapsed on the floor. Jadanne called 911. Paramedics arrived in minutes. But he didn't survive the trip to the hospital.

This is so sudden, so certain, so final. There's little to say on the way home as we nurse our shock and grief.

I call Chuck as soon as I get back to my place. To my surprise and gratitude, he says he'll be here in a few hours. I start talking with Jadanne about funeral arrangements.

Dad was a member of the Burien Elks at one time. Tim followed in his footsteps as a member of the Federal Way Elks Club.

The Elks take charge of planning and organizing the service and reception. They show extraordinary tenderness toward Jadanne and the children left fatherless at fourteen and sixteen years old.

Those we love don't go away. They walk beside us every day. Unseen, unheard, but always near. Still loved, still missed, and forever dear.
—Alex MacLean

One Leaves, One Arrives

My best friends, Elizabeth and Lucy, meet me at the service. In the back of the room, Chuck is dressed in a conservatively smart suit and tie.

"Who's that?" asks Lucy.

"That's Chuck," I respond.

"I thought that was someone from the funeral home," says Elizabeth, having trouble reconciling the man in the back with the skiing boyfriend I've described.

I appreciate that Chuck has gone to the trouble of dressing so respectfully and so handsomely.

A day later, we gather at a river on Mount Rainier near a place where Tim liked to camp. Chuck, Pat, and his son Mike follow Dad as he attempts to reach the river to spread Tim's ashes. Dad's a little unsteady, so Chuck, without saying anything, takes a gentle hold of his arms to keep him from falling into the river.

To recoup some together time from this sad, frantic week, Chuck and I take the next day for a morning of skiing. I drop him off at Sea-Tac to catch his evening flight.

Now I'm with Mom and Dad at their condo. They can't stop talking about Chuck and his quiet, reassuring presence throughout this horrific week. My brother has left the family, and, in a way, Chuck has joined it. I'm sad they never met.

Do you count your losses, appreciate your gains, or do both?

The Adventure Begins

Fall 1980. John R. is in town. Chuck and I meet him at a North End restaurant known for great steaks. We tell him we've decided to get married. He chuckles and asks where and when the wedding will be. I tell him we plan to get married in ski season and that we'll probably just elope.

"Absolutely not!" he says. "You will wear a white wedding dress and get married in a church."

Pushing forty and hardly a virgin, I say, "Would you settle for off-white?"

Mom and Dad are delighted that Chuck and I are getting married. I think Mom had given up on me ever becoming a wife.

We decide that the wedding should be at my church, Seattle Unity, but not the reception. The church basement just isn't our style. I remember a reception Mom raved about, only blocks away. The Sunset Club is a private women's social club. We need a sponsor to have an event there.

I check out The Sunset Club's Board of Directors and see that Dorothy Bullitt, the founder of Seattle's first TV station, is a member. I contact one of her daughters who helped fund the Wing Luke museum, and we have our sponsor.

Mom and I meet with The Sunset Club staff to talk about a reception for a hundred and fifty people. They walk us through and make perfect suggestions for music, food, flowers, and even where the reception line should be.

Mom and Dad want to contribute to the costs.

"Absolutely not!" I say.

Mom objects.

"OK, you can buy the flowers."

And so the adventure called marriage begins!

A Valentine's Day Wedding

It's 1981. We want to get married on a Saturday in February and then skip town on Sunday for our honeymoon at the Banff Sunshine Village ski resort in the Canadian Rockies. We've never been there before.

The second Saturday in February is Valentine's Day. Chuck thinks this is perfect because I'll always remember our anniversary. The night before our wedding, we talk in bed, with tenderness and joy, about our life ahead.

As planned, John R. picks Chuck up from our house for the wedding. He doesn't have a shotgun, at least not that I can see. The ceremony is short and sweet. Chuck claims that our vows said I was to "love, honor, and *obey*" him. However, having been married at Seattle Unity, a contemporary progressive church, I'm certain he remembers wrong.

The reception involves several hours of eating, drinking, dancing, and visiting with our dearest friends and relatives. On Sunday, Mom and Dad host a brunch for immediate family at their condo overlooking Puget Sound. Then we're off to the airport to fly to Calgary.

It's amazing how one day someone walks into your life and suddenly, you can't remember how you lived without them.—Anurag Prakash Ray

Celebration

We stay at the historic Banff Springs Hotel, located at the convergence of the Bow and Spray rivers. Built in 1886 by the Canadian Pacific Railway as one of the most luxurious hotels in the world, some call it the "Castle in the Rockies."

The ski areas at Banff and Lake Louise exceed our expectations. As we travel, we hear Kool and the Gang over and over again singing, "There's a party goin' on right here. A celebration to last throughout the years. So bring your good times and your laughter too. We're gonna celebrate your party with you."

Is there a song you've appreciated for decades?

13
CHAPTER THIRTEEN

Stepping Up

You Never Know Until You Try

July 1983. The morning sun is pounding the sliding glass doors. As I open them, the breeze off the water is welcome. Jim, our next-door neighbor, is having breakfast on his patio, putting up with our kitten, Woolie, who is pestering him for bacon.

Newspaper in hand, Jim leans across the fence, pointing to an article. "I see a judge is retiring," he says. "Are you going to apply for the vacancy?"

I've been thinking about running next year when there'll be an open seat. "I wouldn't have a chance," I say. "The governor's a Republican. I worked on his opponent's campaign."

Just then, Chuck appears with doughnuts and coffee for breakfast on the dock.

"Remember," Chuck says, "this Republican governor bucked his party to nix an oil pipeline running through Washington. He's pretty independent."

Jim, who owns a small business and probably votes Republican himself, agrees. "You should go for it," he says.

Chuck and I continue the discussion privately on the dock. "I'd have to go through the Judicial Evaluation Committee," I point out. "It's almost all men, mostly corporate lawyers from big firms. I'm not sure how I'd do there."

"You never know until you try," Chuck says, his attention now focused on the sports pages.

Nothing is impossible; the word itself says, "I'm possible!"
—*Audrey Hepburn*

Judgment Day

I've completed the ten pages of information required for judicial evaluation. It includes nearly every case I've tried, opposing counsel, and lists of committees and boards. They request awards, papers written, everything except the name of my first Sunday school teacher.

If I run next year for the open seat, I'll have to go through this process anyway, so I might as well face the music now. I'm nervous because I generally represent the little guy. I have a reputation for being independent, prepared, and fearless. The biggest hurdle, of course, is that I'm female. Out of approximately 160 superior court judges in the state, the number of women can be counted on one hand.

I don't know many of the lawyers interviewing me. As they're introduced, I hear the names of some of the most prestigious firms in Seattle.

There are only a few criminal attorneys on the panel, but I'm immediately asked about my criminal experience. I explain that early in my career, I handled routine misdemeanor and felony cases. And that I represented three of seven defendants in a death penalty case where a police officer was killed during a bank robbery. This is an experience few around the table have had, and there are no follow-up questions.

One lawyer asks about the number of jury trials I've handled, as if this is a litmus test of some kind. In addition to the many jury trials I've dealt with, I point out that family law is a significant part of my practice. These cases, especially those involving family-owned businesses, often require trials.

One of the committee co-chairs is a family lawyer. He nods when I add that a family law case requires the same skills as a jury trial except the preparation of jury instructions, because the judge decides the case. I also mention the high percentage of family law cases a King County judge must decide.

Most of the lawyers here represent insurance companies. They're familiar with the Supreme Court decision I recently won abolishing the exclusion that let insurance companies off when one family member injured another.

One of the committee members asks, "In your practice, you primarily represent plaintiffs; can you be fair to defendants and insurers?" I respond that I represented an insurance company for the first three years of my practice. And that I've also represented defendants in trials; I understand both sides.

When I'm asked about my business experience, I talk about having represented businesses ranging from a securities brokerage firm to restaurants, manufacturers, service firms, retail sales, and construction companies.

The toughest question is "Why do you want to be a judge?"

I emphasize that I was raised to be civic-minded and to improve the lives of those around me. But there's so much more that I wonder how I'll work it all into a single coherent response.

I want the judiciary to better reflect the public we serve. I'm committed to improvements that make the system faster, fairer, and less costly. I've been deeply involved in continuing education for lawyers. I'd like to see judges have better continuing education as well. I could go on and on, but I know my time in this interview is short.

I end by saying that while I've enjoyed being an advocate, I look forward to being a neutral decision-maker.

Time flies. I'm out the door in twenty minutes. I think of everything I wish I'd said but didn't. I wonder if I came across as too strident. Whatever the outcome is, it's time to work on the governor.

Judging others is easy because it distracts us from the responsibility of judging ourselves.—Charles Glassman

A Meeting with the Governor

I compile a list of friends I have in common with Governor Spellman. My client and longtime friend, Ruby Chow, was elected to the King County Council when Governor Spellman was county executive. She's on good terms with him. I ask her if she'll write a letter for me. She says, "No, I'll make a call."

Well-known plaintiff's lawyers and defense attorneys write to the governor on my behalf. Prominent citizens and philanthropists who are not lawyers also send letters of support. Rumor has it that two highly placed female judges talk to Lois Spellman on my behalf. The Governor considers his wife his best advisor.

The envelope I've been waiting for arrives. My staff doesn't open it. I use my favorite letter opener and allow relief to flow through my body. The Judicial Evaluation Committee gives me a favorable rating—not the highest rating, but high enough.

I receive a phone call. I have an interview with Governor Spellman in the morning. But I'm scheduled to present a continuing legal education course at a conference near the airport. I quickly arrange to switch my morning slot with one of the afternoon presenters.

Walking up the stairs and through the Corinthian columns, I reach the entrance to the legislative building. The governor's office is on the first floor. The marble, the arches, the dome, and the bronze Tiffany chandeliers soothe my nerves.

I feel nostalgic for the three terms in college when I was on the senate staff. I feel humiliation too, as I remember discovering that I was pregnant "out of wedlock," as we said in those days. With this skeleton in my closet, seeking a judicial appointment is audacious.

Knowing that I'm a less-than-perfect person, I believe I'll be a better judge. I no longer carry my secret with such shame. Giving up my daughter for adoption made me tougher and stronger, two qualities I believe are necessary for being an effective judge.

Judges encounter lying, greed, negligence, and all forms of brutality. They also see abandonment, neglect, familial dysfunction, and the pathos of mental illness. Experiencing my own imperfection endows me with great humility and compassion.

In the reception room, the governor's legal counsel greets me and shows me into his office. The room smells faintly of molasses with a touch of burnt toast from Governor Spellman's pipe smoking.

The governor and I talk of common friends in politics and law. "You're lucky to have Ruby Chow in your corner," he says. I take that as a good sign.

He comments on my pursuit of a degree in tax law: "I like that you're still learning. That's what judges need to be doing all the time."

He asks about my family. I tell him that my husband, Chuck,

is the reason I'm sitting here. I explain what Chuck told me about the pipeline issue and how much I appreciate politicians who take a principled stand on something even when it calls for them to break with their party.

As our conversation wraps up, Governor Spellman says, "I'm inclined to appoint you, but I have to get the official 'clean sheet' from the bar association. You'll probably hear from the press next."

I float out of the room. I think I've just been appointed.

What's the best news you've ever had?

The Call I Can't Wait to Make

The ballroom of the hotel, where our conference is taking place, is packed. I'm glad I prepared well for this lecture; I'm a little distracted by my meeting with the governor. Did he say what I think he said? I haven't told anyone anything yet.

There's a break during my session. Someone rushes up to me saying that Julie Emery, a reporter for *The Seattle Times*, is calling on the hotel line in the hall. Julie congratulates me on my appointment and asks for an interview. I tell her I'm in the middle of a presentation. She says she and a photographer will meet me here after I'm done.

I float back to the speaker's rostrum. I feel the buzz in the room. Word is getting out.

I can't wait to call Chuck.

Bad news travels fast. Good news takes the scenic route.—Doug Larson

Appointed to Serve, Required to Run

It's August. I'm now an appointed judge in King County Superior Court. It's an honor, but a temporary one. State law requires that appointed judges run in a special election in order to serve a full four-year term.

I feel like I'll be running for office forever. Even if I win the special election, I'll run again next year in 1984. Win or lose, I'll serve through January. But I didn't go through all this effort for a five-month assignment.

In no time, the filing period is here for the special election. I file my Declaration of Candidacy at the Elections Department and wait three days to see if anyone files against me.

It's only eight weeks until the election, but we've formed our steering committee. We also have a preliminary budget, a prospective donor list, and a media strategy in the works. This is a county-wide election, and our ultra-thin budget has to cover an area twice the size of Rhode Island.

I draw one opponent, a sixty-eight-year-old man with thirty-eight years of legal practice behind him. Recently, he's been serving as a part-time substitute judge and arbitrator. Although his wife is a well-known East King County realtor, he has limited name recognition.

Our steering committee meets at sunrise before work. "Any idea how hard he'll run?" our treasurer asks. No one seems to know. The newspaper says he ran unsuccessfully once before, twenty years ago. No one knows much else about him.

We strategize about how to approach the campaign. Two people volunteer to help set up newspaper editorial endorsement interviews. One will work with Democrats, the other with Republicans. I have friends in both parties.

With little time and even less money, we realize that our best bet may be signs on Metro buses, which travel the entire county. Someone quickly makes a connection at King County Metro and secures a price we can afford for four weeks of signage. Overnight, someone else creates a logo. Mom and Dad organize volunteers to handle our mailings. Two female lawyers in Pioneer Square host the campaign office. With a simple postcard-type mailer resembling our bus sign, we're off and running for election.

You campaign in poetry. You govern in prose.—Mario Cuomo

An Honor

King County Superior Court judges enter and take their seats at the front of the room with judges from other courts, including one supreme court justice. With Chuck at my side, I couldn't be happier.

The presiding judge makes opening remarks and calls me forward. I raise my right hand and repeat the oath of office in a voice much stronger and more confident than I feel.

Chuck steps forward and dutifully helps me into my black robe. It's an honor he'd gladly forego, but with his parents and mine beaming in the front row, he knows it means a lot to all of us.

Judge Nancy Ann Holman, our first female superior court judge, introduces me. Judge Warren Chan, a mentor and the founder of the Wing Luke museum, speaks about my commitment to diversity. I'm allowed to introduce my family and make brief remarks, but I've been warned to avoid politics.

Have you ever feared being honored?

An Outstanding Reception

Traditionally, a swearing-in ceremony is followed by cookies and coffee in the judge's conference room. In addition, we announced a reception, catered by Ruby Chow, for the many lawyers, judges, politicians, and civic leaders in attendance.

The party is in the Chinese Room on the thirty-fifth floor of the venerable Smith Tower, just a block from the courthouse. When the Smith Tower was built in 1914, it was Seattle's tallest skyscraper.

I underestimate how hard it is to get all the way up to the reception after the cookies and coffee with folks at the courthouse. The Smith Tower still has manually operated elevators to the top floors, so I'm late to my own party. I also underestimate the crowd. Fortunately, Ruby Chow knows how to feed a hungry group.

Even though I've just been sworn in, I'm also running for office. The special election is just a few months away. Fortunately, the big endorsements come in. I pick up an "Outstanding" rating from the respected Municipal League just in time to use it on our bus signs.

If your actions inspire others to dream more, learn more, do more, and become more, you are a leader.—John Quincy Adams

The Hard Part Isn't Winning

My opponent has been largely absent from the campaign. With barely two weeks left until the election, he tells the Bellevue newspaper he hasn't decided whether to spend any money on advertising. "If people want me, they want me. If they don't, they don't," he says.

We're confident but not overconfident that I'll win this election. If I do win, I'll need to run for the full term again next year. How much effort I put into this campaign may determine whether I have an opponent in the next one.

On election night, we have a party at our cottage on the lake. People come and go, bringing generous amounts of food and drink. We won't know the results until the morning, but early returns hint at victory.

Now comes the hard part: doing justice.

> *Injustice anywhere is a threat to justice everywhere.*
> *—Martin Luther King Jr.*

14
CHAPTER FOURTEEN

What Kind of Justice?

New Judge Seeks Justice, Literal and Poetic

August 1983. A judge for two weeks, and now I'm the one seeking justice.

A car rear-ends me in front of a department store and takes off immediately. The police arrive quickly to take statements from witnesses. Some get a few numbers of the license plate.

The impact to my Porsche 914 pushes the rear engine into the back of my seat. Chuck comes and takes me to the ER, where I get X-rays and discover there's nothing broken. A doctor gives me a neck collar and tells me he'll suggest a physical therapist if I'm not better in six weeks. It appears that with repairs, my car may be drivable again.

In September, I see my gynecologist. About six months ago, I went off birth control. I hope Chuck and I get good news confirming my home pregnancy test. He doesn't know yet.

Chuck is shocked when I tell him the news. Even though we talked about it before I went off birth control, I think the reality is just hitting him.

My headaches are still bad, right at the base of the skull. My neck and lower back also hurt. All this sitting as a judge is hard. But I won't take medication while I'm pregnant.

I'm in physical therapy now. I need exercise but want to be careful with the baby coming. I think I'll start doing water aerobics.

I'm beginning to show. But no one notices because of the robe. I wear my coat in the halls as though I'm going outside. I've sworn my staff to secrecy.

I can imagine some of the older, stuffier judges saying something like, "These women. Give them an important job and the first thing they do is get pregnant." Because I'm now forty-one, I also don't want to be very public in case I suffer an early miscarriage.

Christmas parties are coming up, which I'll need to attend because I'm running again next year. I have to get new clothes, but I have to choose a wardrobe that doesn't look like maternity wear.

Have you ever had to hide something obvious?

Prepare Yourself

May 1984. In the last month of my pregnancy, I attend the National Judicial College at the University of Nevada at Reno with eighty new judges from around the country. We don't wear robes here, so my very pregnant condition is obvious.

We discuss how we handle certain things in our respective states. There are so many different procedures and policies, yet somehow justice gets done. While the differences are interesting, our curriculum focuses on the things we have in common: evidence, constitutional law, the basics we learned in law school. The focus is on making proper rulings and preserving records in case of appeal.

There are only four female judges here. Each of us is assigned to a different study group, so we don't get to compare notes.

Tomorrow is Mother's Day. The judges in my study group have a lovely card for the mother-to-be. One more week of judicial college and I head back home.

The baby is due in less than a month. I decided to come here in consultation with my physician. I thought it would be less stressful than being on the bench. But we have so much homework. I've been working all day.

It's late. I finish a long meditation. I've never heard the voice of God speak to me before, but I heard it tonight. The voice said, "Prepare yourself for a great outpouring of love." Chuck and I know this baby will be the greatest outpouring of love we've ever experienced.

I feel cramps, but this must be just false labor. I still have three weeks to go.

The voice you believe will determine the future you experience.
—*Steven Furtick*

Mother's Day

After several restless hours, I'm wide awake. But I know it's too early to begin the day. I check the clock. 5:10 a.m. In addition to the cramping, I'm spotting blood. Now I'm worried.

I dress and head to the lobby to talk to the desk clerk.

"When I came in from the airport, I noticed a hospital nearby," I say. "Can you tell me which way to walk to get there?"

"Sure," he answers. "It's two blocks toward downtown, turn right, and walk two more blocks."

I lumber the four long blocks to the hospital front desk, where I explain my situation. Immediately, I'm taken to a room for an exam.

The nurse performs an ultrasound, rolling the cold ball over my belly. She examines me for a few moments, says nothing, and excuses herself. Within minutes, a doctor appears and repeats the same procedure.

"Am I going to deliver?" I ask him.

He hesitates. "We can't get a heartbeat for the baby," he says.

"What do you mean?" I gasp. "Can you do other tests?"

"I'm sorry," the doctor says. "Your baby is gone. I'm so sorry."

I'm in shock, stunned and silent.

"Is there anyone you want us to call to come and be with you?" the doctor asks.

"I'm here from out of town," I respond frantically. "I need to call my husband and get my doctor's number in Seattle."

They bring a phone into the exam room. I wake Chuck up.

"Chuck," I say. "I need to reach Dr. Hutchison. Can you call him?"

"What do you mean? Are you OK?" he asks.

"No, I'm at the hospital. They say they can't get the baby's heartbeat. I want Dr. Hutchison to talk to the doctor here."

Chuck says he'll call right back.

The wait is agonizing.

The phone rings. It's Chuck.

"Honey, I got ahold of Dr. Hutchison, but you didn't tell me which hospital you were in, so I called the dorm," he says. "The person at the front desk told me you asked for directions to St. Mary's. I gave the number to Dr. Hutchison. He'll call you shortly. I'm going to call for flight information."

Dr. Hutchison calls and talks with the doctor at the hospital. Then he speaks with me. There's nothing to be done.

I'm mute. This can't be happening.

I call my best friend, Elizabeth. We cry together for a bit.

"I need to talk to you about what we do next," says the doctor. "You're going to deliver the fetus, but we know it won't be a live birth. We can make it a much quicker delivery with drugs. We can also give you more pain medication than we would if it were a live birth."

Clinging to a last bit of hope, I ask, "Is there any chance the baby could be resuscitated?"

"No, I'm sorry," the doctor says.

"Let me talk to my husband."

Sobbing again, I dial Chuck.

"They say they're going to induce labor," I tell him. "So it won't take long."

"I've booked a flight," Chuck responds. "I'll be there early this afternoon."

"They say I may be released tonight. There's no need for you to come. I can get a plane home tomorrow."

"Don't be silly," he says. "I'll call you back from the airport while I wait for the plane."

I'm groggy and confused. This can't be happening. It's Mother's Day. Am I being told that because I gave up my daughter so many years ago, I'm unfit to be a mother?

Has the worst day of your life suddenly had to take second place?

What the Voice Meant

I'm taking the week off. Everyone thinks I'm still at judicial college, anyway. Only my staff knows. Chuck is home with me today.

"Honey," I say. "We need to plan a memorial for the baby."

Chuck looks at me with a lost expression.

"Do we have to?" he says.

"I don't feel like it either, but we have to let people grieve with us."

He walks over and puts his arms around me.

"Whatever you want," he says, tears filling his eyes.

I'm crying too.

"We'll keep it very small."

The minister makes mercifully short remarks. We play Jim Croce's "Time in a Bottle" and stand at the back of the chapel, embraced by our closest family members and dearest friends.

I now know that this is what the voice meant when it said, "Prepare yourself for a great outpouring of love."

If I had a box just for wishes and dreams that had never come true...
—Jim Croce

Even Though...

The brass box arrived yesterday.

Today we make the long drive to the Olympic Peninsula. The Pacific Ocean is endlessly gray and grim. With difficulty, Chuck pries the lid off. The wind is raw. We huddle close for the final goodbye to our almost child.

Chuck's dark hair blows across his fair skin, his clear blue eyes sad with regret beyond tears. To give up our tiny child to the force of this vast ocean seems cruel and heartless. Yet we know it's the right thing to do.

The wind seizes handfuls of ashes. We stand together near the dancing surf, bubbling and foamy, dirty, smelling of salt and decay. Buffeted by the ocean wind, we feel small. I'm grateful for the intensity of our embrace as the box empties and the tide takes our only child.

Slowly, we make our way up the sandy switchback path toward our cottage. Deformed pines cling to the desolate hillside. Tall, colorless grasses wave bleakly next to the trail.

Our cottage is musty, and the little kerosene stove is miserly with the heat. We lie together in misery. Chuck strokes my hair and speaks endearments. Tears I thought were all used up come again, but mingled with the sadness this time is gratitude in having such a loving husband. What a fine father he would have made.

Our baby brought us love and such cause for joy. Even though he wasn't alive for even a minute, he enriched the world.

I held you every second of your life.—Stephanie Paige Cole

15
CHAPTER FIFTEEN

Always Running

Supreme Challenge

Spring 1994. I'm doing a two-day executive development workshop at the invitation of my good friend Chris, who works for the organization providing the training. Ever since Chris came to my aid in my first campaign for superior court, I've followed her through a series of positive career moves.

Chris is a great salesperson who always has quality products. I'm sure this workshop will be no different. I'll also have an opportunity to explore my latest goal.

I've enjoyed my time on the King County Superior Court, but my ambition is to become a state supreme court justice. As a superior court judge, I can only dispense justice one case at a time. On the supreme court, I have the opportunity to impact the system as a whole.

In recent years, I've devoted much of my off-duty time to making the court system more effective. Working with other judges, I've introduced computerized individual case management. I've also promoted longer-term assignments to juvenile court to address systemic issues of delinquency, especially with regard to abuse and neglect of children.

In the wake of budget cuts, I've led the group working on the first strategic plan for King County Superior Court to assess our core mission: tightening our belt without adversely affecting justice.

As a superior court judge, I feel I'm rolling a rock uphill as I work for reforms. On the supreme court, though change would still be a challenge, I'd be working from a more consequential vantage point.

My goal seems far off and unlikely. I'm not well known statewide. Although King County has the largest population, there are thirty-eight other counties to consider. Running in a statewide election seems daunting. But is it out of the question? This is what I'm figuring out at this seminar.

> *Sometimes you make the right decision,*
> *sometimes you make the decision right.* —Phil McGraw

What's in a Name?

When I met Chuck, my name was Faith Enyeart. It was difficult to get people to pronounce and spell Enyeart correctly. When we married, I considered taking Chuck's last name, Norem. Wouldn't it be easier to spell? He assured me that people misspelled his name all the time.

I was also a feminist. Keeping my name was to be expected, and Chuck had no objection. I also didn't want to change a well-known King County lawyer's name when I was in practice, so I kept Faith Enyeart and ran for the Superior Court with it.

I always wished I'd had my mother's maiden name, Ireland. Faith Ireland sounds so lyrical! My parents each claimed to be half-French and half-Irish.

I mention to Chuck that this is an odd combination to have on both sides. He says, "Both the French and the Irish hated the British."

Chuck is Norwegian (Viking) on his father's side and Irish on his mother's. His father says, "The Irish are just shipwrecked Vikings."

I'm concerned that Dad might be offended if I change my name to Ireland. He assures me he won't. So in 1992, when Mom celebrates her 75th birthday and I celebrate my 50th, I legally change my name to Faith Enyeart Ireland.

Of course, despite Dad's promise, it's clear that he's hurt by becoming a middle name.

The question now is whether this name change will be a negative or a positive in running statewide for the supreme court.

It's our roots that really give us our identity.—Rosalía

Why Would You Help a Candidate?

It's day two of the workshop. We've covered the skills and competencies of an effective executive. Now we tackle team building.

I tell the group I'm considering a run for the state supreme court. I share my need for a statewide network of people to help with the campaign.

The facilitator asks the group, "Why would someone want to help a candidate for state supreme court justice?" To my surprise, there are many enthusiastic responses.

Carol, a commercial realtor, speaks up: "Knowing what a good judge you've been at the superior court, I might want to help you move up."

Bill, a former teacher, says, "I'd probably help if you got the Washington Education Association endorsement."

Frank, a business owner, says, "I'd be impressed by your integrity and your passion for change in the justice system."

Other participants add more ideas.

Helping others comes easily to me. Asking for help does not. But I need an extraordinary amount of help to run an effective statewide campaign. Experiencing such a generous amount of diverse feedback focuses my thinking about the task ahead by making it more concrete and more manageable.

You miss 100% of the shots you never take.—Wayne Gretzky

Opportunity Knocks. Do I Answer?

It's been six weeks since I completed the executive development workshop. Within the last few days, two long-serving justices, Robert Brachtenbach and James A. Andersen, have announced that they will not be running again for the state supreme court. Both men were former legislators elected as Republicans. They'll serve out their terms through this year, which means there'll be no appointment from the current governor, who is a Democrat.

This morning, I'm having my first "kitchen cabinet" meeting. Most of the people around the table are lawyers. As the campaign moves forward, we'll reach out to a broader constituency.

We discuss the composition of our campaign committee. I get a list of recruitment calls to make. We talk about my chances in the mix of potential candidates. Then, of course, there's the money issue. How can we raise enough to run a statewide campaign?

Our first fundraising effort will be a kickoff breakfast in May, the soonest the law allows us to raise funds. Although breakfasts of this type have been held for charitable events and some partisan political races, they've never been held in a supreme court race. We decide to take a risk.

Have you ever planned a party and asked yourself,
What if no one shows up?

A Sumptuous Breakfast

To prepare for the kickoff breakfast, I work with a consultant who's a former professor at Seattle University and an admired speech writer for state and national leaders. We discuss my ambitions for reform and my personal judicial philosophy. He helps me craft remarks into a short and effective address.

The breakfast is well organized thanks to the tireless efforts of my campaign committee and table captains. My secret weapon has been the volunteer work of my bailiff, Anne, after hours. She's known as a formidable, no-nonsense person.

Anne monitors the table captains, making sure each one has the ten people promised for the 7:30 a.m. breakfast. She also keeps the hotel informed as the numbers jump so it can adjust the room dividers in the ballroom to accommodate the crowd.

I stand at the top of the up escalator at the Westin Hotel to greet guests as they arrive. I'm amazed by the diversity and depth of the turnout: lawyers, neighbors, friends, former clients, many of my superior court colleagues.

After the Pledge of Allegiance and a generous introduction, I take the podium for my first campaign speech. I explain why I'm running and what reforms I believe the supreme court can make to ensure access to justice for all. I end by thanking everyone for coming, especially at such an early hour.

As is the tradition, I leave the room while a pitch for campaign contributions is made. I position myself at the top of the down escalator to thank guests for coming. It's an exhilarating experience of handshakes and hugs.

The breakfast is a huge success, raising over thirty thousand dollars. Equally important, we make a splash in the legal community that confirms my status as a serious candidate. Next comes the chase for endorsements and press coverage, media strategy, and countless evening meetings.

> *Success is not final, failure is not fatal.*
> *It is the courage to continue that counts.* —Winston Churchill

Throwing the Switch

It's a long wait for the end of the filing period in August, which determines the lineup of candidates for each position. I'm running against two men, both judges on the court of appeals. Each is highly distinguished. As a younger female trial court judge, I plan to focus on my differences from the other two highly similar candidates.

The other race is more crowded and boasts a more formidable lineup, including a state senator with good statewide name recognition and a female former superior court judge who also held a position in the Carter administration. I'm grateful not to be running against either of them.

Filing requires paperwork, a trip to Olympia, and a hefty fee that is high enough to discourage frivolous candidates, low enough to be affordable for serious candidates, and proportional to the salary of the position. I show up early on Monday, the first day of filing. I complete my Declaration of Candidacy and fork over the money.

The filing period lasts until Friday. During filing week, it's not uncommon for new candidates to jump into a race or for existing candidates to move from one race to another.

To my horror, this is exactly what happens.

On Wednesday, the female superior court judge with national expertise switches races with one of the court of appeals judges. Now, instead of being the different one, I'm competing against a high-profile woman with judicial and partisan political experience.

When have you needed to make yourself stand out?

Only a Setback

Six weeks later, my worst fears are realized in the primary election. The court of appeals judge wins. I place third out of three.

This is a humiliating defeat. How did I convince myself that I could be a supreme court justice? Worst of all, I've let down the hundreds of people who worked on my campaign.

A few days after the election, I run into my next-door neighbor and leadership mentor, Lou Tice. When he asks how I am, I mention my embarrassing loss. "Only a setback," Lou says cheerfully. I'm surprised and almost offended that he doesn't seem to appreciate the depth of my disaster.

Over the next three months, I busy myself with the duties of my superior court position. But my ego still smarts. However, new opportunities have arisen.

Last month, I was elected to the Washington State Superior Court Judges Association as its first female president. One of my duties as president is serving on the Board for Judicial Administration, which is chaired by the chief justice of the supreme court. This board is responsible for the governance of courts at all levels. My position gives me an opportunity to pursue some of the reforms I care about.

Lou Tice's words echo loudly in my ears.

Being defeated is often a temporary condition.
Giving up is what makes it permanent. —Marilyn vos Savant

16
CHAPTER SIXTEEN

Pain and Promise

Working Through the Pain

Fall 1997. Today, I begin with a personal injury case. The plaintiff was rear-ended and is suffering back pain, headaches, and other symptoms. Sounds familiar.

I'm still having occipital headaches, as well as shoulder, back, and sciatic pain from the hit-and-run I experienced two weeks after becoming a judge. I've tried many things to overcome the pain, from physical therapy and exercises to meditation and biofeedback. I do my best never to show my symptoms while on the bench.

It's voir dire, where lawyers assess the ability of potential jurors to serve fairly. A man is asked about his own back injury from a car accident. He claims he overcame his injury with weightlifting. I tried that, too, but it didn't work.

Then he says something that piques my interest: "I had to disobey my doctor's orders to lift only up to the point of pain."

My doctor said that as well.

But then, this potential juror said something I hadn't heard or even considered: "I found that I had to work through the pain."

At the end of the day, I contact my physical therapist and ask for a referral to a gym close to the courthouse. He suggests one but says, "I have to warn you. This place is a magnet for powerlifters."

"No problem," I respond. "I'll stay out of their way."

When has disobedience helped you?

Something I've Wanted

When I stayed at the Florence Crittenton Home years ago, they provided a safe and private environment for unwed pregnant women like me until we gave birth and put our babies up for adoption.

The Florence Crittenton Home is now a school where teen mothers receive support, academic education, counseling, and parenting skills to raise a healthy family. Young fathers also receive parenting education and support to help their families build a pathway to stability and future success.

Today, I contact a staff member at the Florence Crittenton High School to see if I can get some missing information for my registration with the Colorado Voluntary Adoption Registry. I want the name of the hospital where I gave birth, which I long ago repressed. A case worker I speak with says she thinks she can retrieve my records.

The Colorado Voluntary Adoption Registry helps adoptees and birth parents reconnect if both so desire. I initially filled out an adoption registration form ten years ago when my birth daughter would have turned twenty-two. I waited until then because I wanted her to be the age I was when I made the tough decision to give her up.

I don't know if my daughter knows about the adoption registry or if she has any interest in making contact with me. I don't even know if she's alive and well.

I don't look back on my decision as wrong. Had I kept my daughter in 1965, she would have been stigmatized at that time as a "bastard child." For me, becoming a lawyer would have been impossible. My status as an unwed mother (considered a serious character defect at the time) would surely have disqualified me. Most of all, I wanted my daughter to have both a mother and a father like I had.

For the last ten years, this reunion has been something I've wanted badly. All I can do is hope that my daughter wants it too.

A birth mother always puts the needs of her child above the wants of her heart.—Unknown

Endorphins Kicking In

When I begin weightlifting, I have to drag myself to the gym. One day, I run into one of the young, enthusiastic trainers and ask him why he always seems so happy to be there.

He looks at me in shock. "You mean you aren't?" he asks. I instantly know that loving to work out is a choice like everything else.

A few days later, I'm driving home after an unusually vigorous session of lifting. All of a sudden, a smile comes to my face. I wonder why. It quickly occurs to me that it's the endorphins kicking in.

Endorphins, the happy fitness drug you can never have too much of.
—Unknown

Is This It?

November 10, 1997. It's Monday. I have a raging sinus infection, one of a continuing series. But I also have a murder case in my court, so staying home sick this week is not an option.

During lunch hour, my bailiff says my husband is on the line, a rarity. "You got a call from Theresa at the Colorado Adoption Registry," Chuck tells me. "I have the number here. Do you think this is it?"

"Probably not," I sigh. "They're just looking for more details."

But when I return the call, I discover that this *is* it.

The caseworker in Denver gives me a New York telephone number for a woman named Emily Ann Cantrell. As sick as I'm feeling today, and as little time as I have left in my lunch hour, I hesitate to call, but I can't restrain myself.

I dial the number. A young man picks up. I explain who I am.

"Emily can't talk on the phone right now," he tells me. "She's very emotional and would like to collect herself."

I know the feeling. I leave my numbers.

I have a sleepless night, but strangely, I wake feeling better. I can breathe.

On Wednesday evening, I get a call from New York but not from Emily. It's a friend of hers named Linda.

Linda explains that Emily is overcome with emotion. She wants to be able to collect herself before she talks with me.

Linda tells me a bit about my daughter, speaking of her friend with great affection. Emily is an artist. She has a studio in Manhattan and an apartment in Brooklyn. She works at a Michelin three-star restaurant to support herself.

Knowing that Emily needs time before she feels like talking, I ask Linda if she thinks Sunday might work. That's the best day for me anyway. Linda says she'll check with Emily to make sure.

On Friday, I get a letter with a picture of Emily. I study the picture carefully. I see a tall, slender, dark-haired, dark-eyed beauty with a serious face holding a single large sunflower.

Is this my daughter? I don't see much of a resemblance. Have they made the right match? I'm sure they have, but I'm holding my breath for a flash of recognition.

Finally, it's time for our Sunday call.

Emily apologizes for being too overwhelmed to talk that first day.

"A mundane Monday afternoon turned into a day I'll remember for the rest of my life," she says. "I needed just a little time to let your realness set in before I began considering all the questions I've had in my mind for years. I want you to know how grateful I am to discover that you were looking for me. Somehow I felt that you were."

Along with the shame I felt as an unwed mother in the 1960s, there was also the fear that my adopted child would live a life scarred by rejection, thinking she was unwanted. Emily makes it clear that she respects my decision and is grateful for the life she's lived, growing up in a loving household with two parents, an adopted brother, and an adopted sister.

A rush of relief liberates me.

"This is a huge moment for both of us," Emily says. "Your name is like the cover of a book I've always dreamed about, one that contains deeply personal information and was written just for me."

Ever thought a book was written just for you?

Discoveries Within Discoveries

Today, I receive an email from Emily with another photo attached. Chuck goes to the store for special photo paper and prints it out beautifully before I get home.

I'm pleased that he takes the time to do this, because it shows me that he, too, is excited about this development in my life. His understanding is so important to me.

One look at this photo and I see my daughter.

Standing in front of a giant art installation, wearing a fluffy white sweater and a huge smile, it could be me twenty years ago. Although she has my mom's brown eyes, she has my dark brown hair, smile, and cheekbones. She and I both have a straight, slender nose known in our family as the "Enyeart beak," named for my father. A thrill courses through me. There's no doubt at all now that Emily Ann Cantrell is my daughter.

Now that I'm certain, I go to my parents' condo and interrupt their Thursday night Seinfeld episode to give them the news. Dad says, with tears in his eyes, "I always knew you'd find your daughter. I just didn't know if it would be in my lifetime." We make plans for how we want to share the news with the whole family.

Emily and I establish a routine of talking on the phone on Sundays with email updates in between. We cover the basics, gradually catching up on our thirty-two years apart. We confess our fears about who the person would be. We both realize that our trepidations were wildly exaggerated; we need not have worried at all.

The more we get to know each other, the more we know there is to learn. Like Russian matryoshka dolls, discoveries nest within discoveries. We plan for Emily to meet me and my family in Seattle in January.

Like branches on a tree, we all grow in different directions, yet our roots remain as one.—Suzy Kassem

The Hug We've Been Waiting For

At Sea-Tac Airport, my bouquet of twenty-four long-stemmed red roses commands attention and draws questions from people waiting. When Emily emerges from the plane, we melt into the hug we've been waiting thirty-two years to share. People clap.

A professional photographer, Emily has a few cameras with her, including a mini instant camera, which Chuck uses to take the first picture of mother and daughter. Emily is in the foreground. I'm looking on: one part amazement, two parts curiosity, ninety-seven parts love.

Before the weekend is over, Emily meets the whole Enyeart tribe, my bailiff, and my trainer. She also meets Spook and Spot, our twin white cats, and Millie and Tasha, our neighbor's dogs.

Back home in Brooklyn, Emily emails to say she's been showing off pictures of me "like the proud parent of a newborn." We begin making plans for me to visit her in New York and meet her family in Denver, as well as for us to get together with Chuck's family in Arizona. Everyone is excited about how our family has grown.

All that we love deeply becomes a part of us.—Helen Keller

Still Staying Out of Their Way?

I'm diligent about my workouts.
I train with a young woman in the evenings but find out that she now has to switch to mornings. Not a time I can make.

One of the gym's owners is Willie Austin, a well-known former University of Washington football player and world champion powerlifter. I ask if he'd be willing to coach me even though I'm not a powerlifter. He says he'd love to.

Little do I know that I'll soon become a powerlifter myself and the Chair of the Austin Foundation, providing free fitness training to inner-city youth.

Be careful who you hang with!

17
CHAPTER SEVENTEEN

Once Bitten, Twice Shy?

Raised to Follow My Dreams

January 1998. James Dolliver, Chief Justice of the Washington State Supreme Court, is retiring. An Associated Press reporter calls to ask if the rumors that I'm running for the court are true. I'm looking into it, I tell him. I'll decide in February.

Of course, Chuck is the first person I need to talk to. As always, he says he'll support me if I choose to run again.

I once told a psychiatrist friend that I could see myself either highly successful in my practice, holding high public office, or happily married. I told him how I could see myself as the woman behind the man or in an elected position, but not both.

He said, "You've got it wrong. You need to marry someone who will be the man behind the woman." Lucky for me, my husband, Chuck, is that man. But do I choose to run again?

Next stop, Mom and Dad.

I visit on Seinfeld night and wait for the show to end. I tell Mom I'm considering another run for the supreme court.

"Oh, honey, do you have to?" she asks. "Can't you be satisfied with everything you've already achieved? And what about Emily? If the press gets a hold of the story, it could be bad for both of you."

"Let them get a hold of it," I respond. "I already have the pro-choice vote. A story about the daughter I gave up for adoption, instead of having an abortion, might get me the pro-life vote too."

Raising her maternal shield, Mom says, "I just don't want to see you hurt."

"I understand, Mom," I reply. "But you've always raised us to follow our dreams, and this one is mine. So it's really your fault that I want to try again."

What can she say?

"If that's what you really want, your dad and I will be there for you."

When your values are clear to you, making decisions becomes easier.
—Roy Disney

Eyes Wide Open

A good friend and big supporter of mine in the last campaign drops by my chambers to check out the rumor that I'm running. I tell him that I'm close to an announcement. He says I shouldn't bother because another candidate has the race sewn up.

The candidate's name is Hugh Spitzer. He's a municipal bond lawyer in a large Seattle law firm. He's also a constitutional scholar and adjunct professor at the University of Washington School of Law.

"Look," my friend says, "Hugh has already raised a hundred thousand dollars and has endorsements from county and city leaders all over the state. If you get into this race, you'll just be wasting your time and money."

I thank him for coming by.

It's time to decide.

What about my loss last time around? Will that be a handicap? When I worked in politics as a teenager, men who lost almost always ran again.

Bob Greive, one of my early mentors, was beaten after sixteen years in the state senate, much of that as majority leader. Then he ran for county council and won. He earned double his state senator's salary and didn't have to drive a hundred-and-twenty-mile round trip to Olympia all the time. He served with distinction, making particular contributions on county bus transportation issues. His loss was truly a kick upstairs.

Running for the supreme court the first time was like diving off a cliff blindfolded. I had no idea what I'd find at the bottom. This time, I'm jumping with no blindfold and my eyes wide open.

You can't make decisions based on fear and the possibility of what might happen.—Michelle Obama

It's All Business

I choose to follow my dream.

The first time I ran for the supreme court was exciting and exhilarating. This time it's all business.

One of my most important female mentors, now a federal judge, tells me where she thinks I went wrong last time. She makes a number of strategic recommendations, particularly about endorsements. Her suggestions go to the top of my list.

Anne Bremner, a high-powered trial lawyer and former prosecutor, agrees to be my campaign treasurer. She's well connected in the Republican party. Anne has a million ideas for how to win this time. A few people like Anne who really believe in me will make a huge difference this time around.

Now that I've decided to run, life swirls around me. Meeting with key people, trying cases, and staying fit is daunting. I can't do it all. So I concentrate on the critical 20 percent.

January flies by, and my life is no longer my own. I'm now an official candidate. I'm still serving on the superior court. But now every breakfast, lunch, and dinner is spoken for.

As a public servant, I can't campaign from my chambers. I can't use public resources or any staff during their working hours. But I have a membership in a club with an elegant restaurant and conference rooms only a block away. I rush over there when I need to make calls or meet with people.

The old excitement returns. A good meeting with a fundraiser helps. In this case, the term "fundraiser" is a bit misleading. These people help me develop a strategy for raising funds, but they don't raise money themselves.

Unlike candidates for other types of races, judicial candidates aren't allowed to solicit funds from anyone personally. We must recruit a fundraising committee to do the asking.

I have my first campaign meeting tomorrow afternoon with a small group of ten to fifteen volunteers. From this group, we'll develop our official steering committee.

Yes we can!—Barack Obama

Behind, Bewildered, Beholden—Be Tough!

The daffodils are coming in early, beating their usual March arrival by two weeks. By contrast, I feel like my campaign is running behind, as my opponent has his full campaign committee in place and his staff hired.

Chuck and I contributed fifty thousand dollars to the last campaign. I have informed my campaign committee that, other than a modest donation from my family, this year's campaign will only be able to eat what it kills.

I can't outspend my opponent. But in judicial races, money isn't everything. In a statewide campaign, it's hard for even well-financed candidates to reach voters in truly affordable ways.

What we can count on is a voter's pamphlet statement with my biography delivered as an insert with each local newspaper before the primary.

Candidates finishing first and second in the primary get a voter's pamphlet statement for the general election. This is the single most important item in the campaign. Crafting it is one of my highest responsibilities.

Other candidates have advantages over me. But the fact that I'm already a judge outweighs many of these things. Voters want to know that a member of the supreme court has public trust based on former judicial, legislative, or other service requiring accountability.

I meet my opponent for the first time. He's not a trial lawyer, so he's never appeared in my court. I doubt that I'll disagree much with Hugh Spitzer on public policy. But there are rumors of other candidates jumping in who differ sharply.

Tomorrow is Valentine's Day, and Chuck and I are celebrating our seventeenth wedding anniversary. We didn't get reservations in time for our favorite restaurant, so we celebrate with another couple at home. Even with all the campaign mayhem, celebrating Chuck as my number-one supporter is at the top of my list.

The travel requirements of a statewide campaign are exhausting and often frustrating.

I head north to Lynnwood for a meeting, but another group has the space reserved. Fog in Spokane causes me to miss a flight and a luncheon with the dean of Gonzaga Law School. I also miss a meeting with a possible campaign volunteer for Spokane County.

Tomorrow, I speak at Seattle University Law School about the duties of judges, the code of judicial conduct, and elections.

I can't believe I have a free evening tomorrow night. Does this mean that even with the good networking of my eagle-eyed campaign staff, I'm probably missing something?

No such thing as spare time, no such thing as free time, no such thing as down time. All you got is life time. Go.—Henry Rollins

Like a Wind-Up Toy

I've been up until all hours completing twenty-page questionnaires for two bar association endorsing groups. Endorsement interviews follow in a few weeks.

The campaign is a blur. I feel like a toy my handlers wind up every morning with the day's schedule and instructions.

I have an interview with law enforcement unions from around the state on Friday. On Saturday, I head north to Skagit County to speak to both the Democratic and Republican County Conventions.

It's two weeks until our kickoff breakfast. My committee has been hard at work recruiting table captains. Once again, Anne, my former bailiff who now works for a law firm, has taken charge.

Tomorrow is an early-morning kickoff breakfast for a prosecutor followed by a drive to Tacoma to tape a cable public service television program on landlord-tenant matters. Finally, I drive another two hours to Ocean Shores for a judges' conference and back again at night.

Today I'm in the charming Bavarian town of Leavenworth in the Cascade Mountains to give an educational presentation at the Young Lawyers Convention. This afternoon, it's back to Seattle to officiate at a wedding. Tonight I'm attending the National Organization of Women auction.

I'll devote Sunday to reviewing press releases and working on my speech for the kickoff breakfast. If time permits, I'll get to church, do a quick workout, and have my nails done.

Have you ever felt like a wind-up toy?

For the First Time

The kickoff breakfast is a great success, with more than three hundred in attendance. I don't have the final figures, but I'm sure we made our fundraising goal.

Today I arrive home to find long-stemmed pink roses and a Mother's Day card from Emily. Tomorrow is Mother's Day, and for the first time, I'm a mother!

Being reunited with my birth daughter has helped me to heal from not only her loss but the loss of our son on Mother's Day as well.

In recent years, I've hidden out on this day, but tomorrow I'll celebrate with Mom and talk to Emily in Brooklyn.

A mother's love is more beautiful than any fresh flower.
—Debasish Mridha

A New Kind of Optimism

It's June, and the mania of campaigning at such a hectic pace is wearing me down. I also feel I'm being outdone by my toughest opponent, Hugh Spitzer. I remind myself that these campaigns are unpredictable. Chuck keeps my spirits up.

In my last campaign, I had thousands of flyers printed at a considerable cost. This time, I use a bi-fold business card with credentials and contact information. I prepare copies of a customized letter for each event I attend. I help set up chairs. I pass out my own literature. There's no "advance man" or pampering for me in this race.

Both of my parents are failing. Dad has Alzheimer's. Mom, frail and underweight, has pneumonia. I feel guilty that I'm not spending more time with them. Fortunately, my brother, who is now retired, has returned from wintering in Arizona and is pitching in.

This time around, campaigning feels like childbirth. Had I recalled all that it requires, I would surely have passed on doing it again. But as Chuck reminds me, "The only thing that would make you more miserable than campaigning would be not campaigning."

Chuck pulls me out of my morass. This is no time to feel anxious, depressed, or guilty about my parents.

I also get a boost from my friend Dan, an executive leadership expert. In a brief conversation, I share my fears with him. He shares with me some timely wisdom.

Dan sends me out to buy a book called *Learned Optimism* by Martin Seligman (the father of the positive psychology movement), which I dutifully read. Our two-hour meeting is exciting, revealing, and exactly the kind of makeover I need.

In July, I'm back on a roll. I receive the sole endorsements of the State Firefighters' Council and all the significant state police organizations. These endorsements are critical because voters tend to think female judges will be too sympathetic in criminal cases.

Both Hugh Spitzer and I have been endorsed by the Washington Education Association. He'll clean up on the newspaper endorsements. But now, thanks to Dan (and Martin Seligman), I have a new kind of optimism from which I draw energy and hope.

Creativity is bound up in our ability to find new ways around old problems.—Martin Seligman

Seven Candidates, One Position

Friday, July 31, 1998. The filing deadline passes. It's a large field now, with seven candidates in the race. Three of us have been campaigning for months; the other four just hopped in. A reporter tells me that two of them are out of state on vacation. They're probably not serious candidates.

A few years ago, a relatively unknown lawyer beat an incumbent justice. Ever since, there's been a kind of lottery mentality about these races. For the $1,181 filing fee, you get a one-in-seven chance this time at a six-year job with a salary of $110,000 a year, retirement benefits, and incredible prestige. Any publicity along the way is good for a candidate's law practice even if they don't get elected.

Actually, I think the crowded field works to my advantage. I'm now clearly the distinctive candidate: the only one with judicial experience, the only woman, and the only candidate endorsed by all of the statewide law enforcement groups.

I'm holding a vision of being sworn into the supreme court with my daughter Emily there to help me don my robe. Chuck did this for me when I was sworn into the superior court. But, being an introvert, he will gladly give up the spotlight.

With seven candidates, this is a complicated race. It's more competitive, to be sure, but I see a clearer path to victory. However, one of the candidates who entered at the last minute troubles me a bit because he has a famous name.

James Patrick "Jim" Foley is in no way related to Tom Foley from Spokane, a famous Washington politician and lawyer. Tom Foley is a former speaker of the US House of Representatives and is now our ambassador to Japan.

Jim Foley doesn't have any credentials like these, but he's a likely choice for voters who don't study judicial races closely and may be easily confused. I know that worrying about this isn't helpful, but I worry about it nonetheless.

Chuck's job description in our marriage has always boiled down to "Now, calm down." I hear it every time I land like a helicopter after an exciting, exhilarating, combative, frustrating day in court or on the campaign trail. His calm and reassuring voice always soothes me.

I need him now more than ever. He helps me manage the stress of campaigning, the extensive travel, and my existing superior court workload.

I've chosen to follow a demanding dream, but I know I have everything I need: a wonderful husband, supportive parents, and, at long last, a daughter!

Who are the people in your life you are most grateful for?

Recognition Comes and Goes

I attend a conference on judicial education at Port Ludlow on the Olympic Peninsula, where the Leadership Institute of Judicial Education presents me with the Distinguished Service Award. The award recognizes my more than ten years of helping to raise the level of judicial education in over forty states.

But just as quickly, I feel overlooked and underappreciated. *The Seattle Times* runs an article about my race, full of speculation about whether Hugh Spitzer or Kris Sundberg will win. I don't even get a mention.

Anne Bremner and I sit in the August sunshine on my patio above the lake, strategizing about how to take back the campaign in the Seattle newspapers. Fortunately, it's vacation season, and readership is down. Even people reading their papers don't have their minds on the September 16 primary. In Seattle—rain city—August is that time of year when being outdoors matters more than politics.

Elections belong to the people. It's their decision. If they decide to turn their back on the fire and burn their behinds, then they will just have to sit on their blisters.—Abraham Lincoln

18
CHAPTER EIGHTEEN

Getting to Justice

Supreme Choice

Fall 1998. I've been blessed with two campaign media wizards, one Democrat and one Republican. Both have come on board as volunteers. Although they usually work on opposing sides, this is not their first joint effort. They worked together in support of the Solidarity movement to promote free elections in Poland.

They estimate that mounting a media-driven campaign that would truly affect voters in a statewide nonpartisan race might cost as much as three-quarters of a million dollars. But the most that has ever been spent in a supreme court campaign is approximately $400,000. And that candidate lost to an opponent who spent less than $50,000. We need to come up with a strategy to leverage the limited funds we have in the most meaningful way possible.

We decide to run newspaper ads to get the most bang for our buck. We choose the five most widely read newspapers around the state and decide to run full- or half-page ads depending on circulation. All will appear on the same day, halfway between the time absentee ballots are sent and in-person voting day.

My media strategy team gains an unlikely new consultant when my husband, Chuck, who normally stays in the background, has a great idea for the ads.

Chuck's idea is to use a large picture of me in judicial robes with the headline "SUPREME CHOICE!" and brief bullet points that describe my experience, my proven leadership abilities, and the key endorsements I've received.

The ad then says, "OR..." and has six small boxes, each with the same male silhouette and a question mark. Under the pictures, the text notes that none of them has ever been a judge.

At the bottom is a simple message: "It's anybody's guess how these politicians, professors, or lawyers with familiar-sounding names would perform on our state's highest court. But you can elect a real judge, Judge Faith Ireland."

There's a lot of talk about our ads. We know they aren't likely to affect the outcome, but the buzz from political insiders may. Finally, we look like a front-runner.

How do you decide who you will vote for?

The Newspapers Have a Laugh at My Expense

The September 16 primary comes quickly enough, and the results show how little *The Seattle Times* knew about the race. The candidates they favored, Spitzer and Sundberg, come in fourth and third respectively. I come in second and advance to the general election.

Jim Foley, the man with the famous name, captures all the day-after press. Almost every newspaper features a photo of Foley dressed in a white shirt, a colorful tie, and suspenders. He's known for his loud belly laugh and, in the context of this race, his powerful name recognition.

In an article titled "Laughter in the Court," *The Seattle Times* reports that "Foley is an unknown with a famous last name. He filed for office and took a vacation. He didn't bother to put up a campaign sign and didn't tell friends or even his mother-in-law that he was running."

With the primary his, Foley tells the media that he has already written the headline for the day after the November 3 election: "Irishman Upsets Ireland."

When our campaign steering committee meets, we agree that we're all relieved that the general election will not be against the well-respected and well-funded Hugh Spitzer. We also agree not to take Jim Foley lightly in any way.

All five past presidents of the pre-eminent plaintiffs' and civil defendants' bar associations have sent a letter on my behalf to all the trial lawyers in the state. They care deeply about who is on our state supreme court. The letter says, in part, "We seldom agree on much, but on this we do agree: judges on the Washington State Supreme Court should be experienced. Judge Faith Ireland has the requisite experience; Mr. Foley does not."

Our campaign also gets a bump when Governor Gary Locke agrees to join as an honorary campaign chair along with former Governors John Spellman, a Republican, and Albert Rosellini, a Democrat. Although Governor Locke does not normally endorse judicial candidates, he's making an exception for this race.

You need fans in high places, I always tell people.
I don't care how talented you are. —Jaleel White

The Elk Meat Constituency

Jim Foley and I meet for the first time when he shows up for an editorial board interview at *The Yakima Herald-Republic*. Between interviews, we pass with a nod and a perfunctory handshake.

Foley and I have our first debate in Vancouver, WA, before the League of Women Voters and the Clark County Bar Association. As he seems to do everywhere, Foley talks up his traits as a good father, a good man, a good lawyer, and a relatable small-town guy. I, too, grew up in a small town (Burien, WA), but I'm regarded as the big-city candidate.

We're both asked how we've helped improve access to the justice system for those who lack financial resources and social capital. I mention my free legal services, including my work on a first-degree aggravated murder case. In his predictably folksy way, Mr. Foley counters, "I've been paid in fish; I've been paid in elk meat." Since then, newspapers have pointed out that a payment of six hundred pounds or more of elk meat may constitute a felony.

Tonight, with fifteen days to go until the general election, my opponent and I appear at a League of Women Voters Forum at the University of Washington School of Law. Once again Foley touts his small-town "common man" values, but he doesn't mention elk meat.

The object of government in peace and in war is not the glory of rulers or of races but the happiness of the common man.—William Beveridge

My Brother to the Rescue

An ambulance takes Dad to Swedish Hospital with a ruptured colon. Given his dementia, he's having a hard time following what's happening to him. I now refer to the hospital as my Capitol Hill campaign headquarters.

My brother Pat is working to move Mom into an assisted living facility in Federal Way, near where he lives in the summer. Thank goodness he's retired and able to spend all this time with our parents.

Nobody cares how much you know until they know how much you care.
—Theodore Roosevelt

When You've Given Your All

Our steering committee decides to do a one-day newspaper blitz like we did in the primary. My media strategist wants to change the format now that I have a known opponent, but after talking with Chuck, I resolve to stick with the same format. Why mess with what works?

With less than two weeks to go, I collect most of the newspaper endorsements. One of the Seattle dailies writes that "Foley's run has had too much of the lark about it, and we like to see campaigns displaying more solid stuff. Ireland has earned the respect, the trust, and the votes of the state's citizens."

Of course, if newspaper endorsements truly mattered, Hugh

Spitzer would have won the primary instead of coming in fourth. These endorsements don't carry the weight they once did, but it's certainly better to have them than not.

It's the Friday before the Tuesday election. There's bad news in the polling. Apparently, a question about my race was included in a poll I knew nothing about. A friend tells me that the poll results indicate that if the election were held today, I'd lose. He wants me to do a last-minute media blitz over the weekend. I thank my well-meaning friend and wait for Chuck to get home.

Chuck and I discuss it and decide to do nothing. We know we've given the campaign our all. We'll let Providence take it from here.

When have you given something your all even with uncertainty?

Anything Can Happen

As usual, the Westin Hotel in downtown Seattle hosts an election-night extravaganza. The grand ballroom is the televised media headquarters. Campaigns have suites and conference rooms for their committees. Candidates, supporters, and the press circulate, awaiting the display of early results.

As Chuck and I take the escalator up to the ballroom, a reporter says, "Congratulations, Justice Ireland." We haven't seen any votes yet, but his comment is encouraging. He photographs us with fingers crossed.

As we reach the ballroom, we see the first results of my race. Most of the votes have yet to be counted, but I'm doing well. Confident but not overconfident, I know that anything can happen. If it's a close race, I may have to wait several days for absentee ballots to be counted.

Two hours later, we're across the street at The Mayflower Hotel in a suite that my friend Joan and her partner Steve have rented for our after-party. It's almost midnight; we'll soon have the last results of the day. I wait, holding my breath. Steve, holding the champagne, waits to pop the cork.

The midnight numbers arrive. I'm winning with nearly 60 percent of the vote, a decisive victory.

The crowd cheers, champagne glasses fill, and Steve makes a toast: "Here's to Justice Faith Ireland!"

Gratitude, relief, elation, and a flood of other reactions compete in a jumble of thoughts ricocheting inside of me. I'm honored to have been selected by the voters. I'm proud of my campaign staff and of myself, too, for proving worthy of their enormous support. I've erased the loss of my first embarrassing supreme court campaign. I've followed my dream and redeemed myself in its fulfillment.

Don't give up on your dreams, or your dreams will give up on you.
—John Wooden

A Thanksgiving Celebration

We move Dad from the hospital to a nursing home. Finally, he's in the Alzheimer's wing of the assisted living unit. Mom now has an apartment in the same building and a Lhasa Apso dog named Millie.

Thanksgiving is a joyful affair at my brother Pat's home. We spring Dad and load him, his wheelchair and walker, Mom, and Millie, too, into Chuck's jeep.

Dad has a good day, thoroughly enjoying himself. Though he isn't aware of it, he recently received his forty-five-year certificate from the National Plumbers and Pipe Fitters Union. Pat makes a formal presentation with a toast, celebrating Dad for his accomplishment and me for mine.

What is your most memorable Thanksgiving?

My Place Among the Nine

It's January 11, 1999. I'm 56.

A crowd fills the grand foyer of the Temple of Justice in Olympia, where the Washington State Supreme Court convenes. Dignitaries, friends, family, and supporters of the justices to be sworn in enter through massive brass doors.

Someone takes a picture of our three generations of women: Mom, tiny, stooped, and frail, but looking up with effort and a smile; me, happy and healthy; my daughter, Emily, statuesque and striking. I'm so grateful life has allowed Mom to see her daughter realize a dream and to know her beautiful granddaughter.

Before we enter the courtroom, we meet in the reception room, where I welcome former Governor John Spellman and his wife, Lois, and other state officials, including attorney general, Christine Gregoire, and governor, Gary Locke.

Governor Spellman, who originally appointed me to the superior court, tells me he's proud to have been invited to make my formal introduction after I'm sworn in. I thank him for starting me on my judicial career with his appointment.

Emily, Chuck, and I are ushered into the front row. Mom and other family members sit a few rows back. The chief justice offers welcoming remarks. Senior justices who have been re-elected are sworn in.

I'm called to step forward, raise my hand, and pledge to uphold the constitution and laws of the State of Washington and the United States. The chief justice announces that my daughter, Emily Cantrell, of Brooklyn, New York, will assist me in donning my judicial robe.

Looking every bit like a New York fashion model, Emily elegantly slides the gown over my shoulders. I manage the zipper even though my hands tremble with nervous excitement.

I'm now ushered to the bench, where I shake hands with each justice as I pass and take my seat on the supreme court.

With each hand clasped, circles close: mother to daughter, lawyer to justice, private citizen to public servant, underestimated woman to esteemed colleague.

It's been a long road getting to justice. At last, I take my place among the nine.

Never forget that justice is what love looks like in public.—Cornel West

Made in United States
Troutdale, OR
09/05/2024

22625602R00137